Eng^{d}. by A H Ritchie.

Alice Cary

BALLADS, LYRICS, AND HYMNS.

BY

ALICE CARY.

POPULAR EDITION.

NEW YORK:
PUBLISHED BY HURD AND HOUGHTON
Cambridge: Riverside Press.
1876.

RIVERSIDE, CAMBRIDGE:
STEREOTYPED AND PRINTED BY
H. O. HOUGHTON AND COMPANY.

O EVER true and comfortable mate,
  For whom my love outwore the fleeting red
Of my young cheeks, nor did one jot abate,
  I pray thee now, as by a dying bed,
Wait yet a little longer! Hear me tell
  How much my will transcends my feeble powers:
  As one with blind eyes feeling out in flowers
Their tender hues, or, with no skill to spell
  His poor, poor name, but only makes his mark,
  And guesses at the sunshine in the dark,
So I have been. A sense of things divine
  Lying broad above the little things I knew,
The while I made my poems for a sign
  Of the great melodies I felt were true.

Pray thee accept my sad apology,
  Sweet master, mending, as we go along,
  My homely fortunes with a thread of song,
That all my years harmoniously may run ;
  Less by the tasks accomplished judging me,
Than by the better things I would have done.
  I would not lose thy gracious company
Out of my house and heart for all the good
Besides, that ever comes to womanhood, —
  And this is much : I know what I resign,
  But at that great price I would have thee mine.

CONTENTS.

BALLADS.

THOUGHTS AND THEORIES.

List of Illustrations.

Ballads.

THE YOUNG SOLDIER.

INTO the house ran Lettice,
With hair so long and so bright,
Crying, "Mother! Johnny has 'listed!
He has 'listed into the fight!"

"Don't talk so wild, little Lettice!"
And she smoothed her darling's brow,
"'T is true! you'll see — as true can be —
He told me so just now!"

"Ah, that 's a likely story!
  Why, darling, don't you see,
If Johnny had 'listed into the war
  He would tell your father and me!'

"But he is going to go, mother,
  Whether it 's right or wrong;
He is thinking of it all the while,
  And he won't be with us long."

"Our Johnny going to go to the war!"
  "Ay, ay, and the time is near;
He said, when the corn was once in the ground,
  We could n't keep him here!"

"Hush, child! your brother Johnny
  Meant to give you a fright."
"Mother, he 'll go, — I tell you I know
  He 's 'listed into the fight!

"Plucking a rose from the bush, he said,
  Before its leaves were black
He 'd have a soldier's cap on his head,
  And a knapsack on his back!"

"A dream! a dream! little Lettice,
  A wild dream of the night;
Go find and fetch your brother in,
  And he will set us right."

So out of the house ran Lettice,
  Calling near and far, —
"Johnny, tell me, and tell me true,
  Are you going to go to the war?"

At last she came and found him
  In the dusty cattle-close,
Whistling Hail Columbia,
  And beating time with his rose.

The rose he broke from the bush, when he said,
  Before its leaves were black
He 'd have a soldier's cap on his head,
  And a knapsack on his back.

Then all in gay mock-anger,
  He plucked her by the sleeve,
Saying, "Dear little, sweet little rebel,
  I am going, by your leave!"

"O Johnny! Johnny!" low he stooped,
  And kissed her wet cheeks dry,
And took her golden head in his hands,
  And told her he would not die.

"But, Letty, if anything happen —
  There won't! and he spoke more low —
But if anything should, you must be twice as good
  As you are, to mother, you know!

"Not but that you are good, Letty,
As good as you can be;
But then you know, it might be so,
You 'd have to be good for me!"

So straight to the house they went, his cheeks
Flushing under his brim;
And his two broad-shouldered oxen
Turned their great eyes after him.

That night in the good old farmstead
Was many a sob of pain;
"O Johnny, stay! if you go away,
It will never be home again!"

But Time its still sure comfort lent,
Crawling, crawling past,
And Johnny's gallant regiment
Was going to march at last.

And steadying up her stricken soul,
The mother turned about,
Took what was Johnny's from the drawer
And shook the rose-leaves out;

And brought the cap she had lined with silk,
And strapped his knapsack on,
And her heart, though it bled, was proud as she said,
"You would hardly know our John!"

Another year, and the roses
  Were bright on the bush by the door;
And into the house ran Lettice,
  Her pale cheeks glad once more.

"O mother! news has come to-day!
  'T is flying all about;
Our John's regiment, they say,
  Is all to be mustered out!

"O mother, you must buy me a dress,
  And ribbons of blue and buff!
O what shall we say to make the day
  Merry and mad enough!

"The brightest day that ever yet
  The sweet sun looked upon,
When we shall be dressed in our very best,
  To welcome home our John!"

So up and down ran Lettice,
  And all the farmstead rung
With where he would set his bayonet,
  And where his cap would be hung!

And the mother put away her look
  Of weary, waiting gloom,
And a feast was set and the neighbors met
  To welcome Johnny home.

The good old father silent stood,
  With his eager face at the pane,
And Lettice was out at the door to shout
  When she saw him in the lane.

And by and by, a soldier
  Came o'er the grassy hill;
It was not he they looked to see,
  And every heart stood still.

He brought them Johnny's knapsack,
  'T was all that he could do,
And the cap he had worn begrimed and torn,
  With a bullet-hole straight through!

O WINDS! ye are too rough, too rough!
O Spring! thou art not long enough
  For sweetness; and for thee,
O Love! thou still must overpass
Time's low and dark and narrow glass,
  And fill eternity.

RUTH AND I.

It was not day, and was not night;
The eve had just begun to light,
  Along the lovely west,
His golden candles, one by one,
And girded up with clouds, the sun
  Was sunken to his rest.

Between the furrows, brown and dry,
We walked in silence — Ruth and I;
  We two had been, since morn
Began her tender tunes to beat
Upon the May-leaves young and sweet,
  Together, planting corn.

Homeward the evening cattle went
In patient, slow, full-fed content,
  Led by a rough, strong steer,
His forehead all with burs thick set,
His horns of silver tipt with jet,
  And shapeless shadow, near.

2

With timid, half-reluctant grace,
Like lovers in some favored place,
  The light and darkness met,
And the air trembled, near and far,
With many a little tuneful jar
  Of milk-pans being set.

We heard the house-maids at their cares,
Pouring their hearts out unawares
  In some sad poet's ditty,
And heard the fluttering echoes round
Reply like souls all softly drowned
  In heavenly love and pity.

All sights, all sounds in earth and air
Were of the sweetest; everywhere
  Ear, eye, and heart were fed;
The grass with one small burning flower
Blushed bright, as if the elves that hour
  Their coats thereon had spread.

One moment, where we crossed the brook
Two little sunburnt hands I took,—
  Why did I let them go?
I 've been since then in many a land,
Touched, held, kissed many a fairer hand,
  But none that thrilled me so.

Why, when the bliss Heaven for us made
Is in our very bosoms laid,
  Should we be all unmoved,
And walk, as now do Ruth and I,
'Twixt th' world's furrows, brown and dry,
  Unloving and unloved?

HAGEN WALDER.

THE day, with a cold, dead color
  Was rising over the hill,
When little Hagen Walder
  Went out to grind in th' mill.

All vainly the light in zigzags
  Fell through the frozen leaves,
And like a broidery of gold
  Shone on his ragged sleeves.

No mother had he to brighten
  His cheek with a kiss, and say,
" 'T is cold for my little Hagen
  To grind in the mill to-day."

And that was why the north winds
  Seemed all in his path to meet,
And why the stones were so cruel
  And sharp beneath his feet.

And that was why he hid his face
  So oft, despite his will,
Against the necks of the oxen
  That turned the wheel of th' mill.

And that was why the tear-drops
  So oft did fall and stand
Upon their silken coats that were
  As white as a lady's hand.

So little Hagen Walder
  Looked at the sea and th' sky,
And wished that he were a salmon,
  In the silver waves to lie;

And wished that he were an eagle,
  Away through th' air to soar,
Where never the groaning mill-wheel
  Might vex him any more:

And wished that he were a pirate,
  To burn some cottage down,
And warm himself; or that he were
  A market-lad in the town,

With bowls of bright red strawberries
  Shining on his stall,
And that some gentle maiden
  Would come and buy them all!

So little Hagen Walder
  Passed, as the story says,
Through dreams, as through a golden gate,
  Into realities.

And when the years changed places,
  Like the billows, bright and still,
In th' ocean, Hagen Walder
  Was the master of the mill.

And all his bowls of strawberries
  Were not so fine a show
As are his boys and girls at church
  Sitting in a row!

Among the pitfalls in our way
  The best of us walk blindly;
O man, be wary! watch and pray,
  And judge your brother kindly.

Help back his feet, if they have slid,
  Nor count him still your debtor;
Perhaps the very wrong he did
  Has made yourself the better.

OUR SCHOOLMASTER.

WE used to think it was so queer
  To see him, in his thin gray hair,
Sticking our quills behind his ear,
  And straight forgetting they were there.

We used to think it was so strange
  That he should twist *such* hair to curls,
And that his wrinkled cheek should change
  Its color like a bashful girl's.

Our foolish mirth defied all rule,
  As glances, each of each, we stole,
The morning that he wore to school
  A rose-bud in his button-hole.

And very sagely we agreed
  That such a dunce was never known —
Fifty! and trying still to read
  Love-verses with a tender tone!

No joyous smile would ever stir
  Our sober looks, we often said,
If we were but a Schoolmaster,
  And had, withal, his old white head.

One day we cut his knotty staff
  Nearly in two, and each and all
Of us declared that we should laugh
  To see it break and let him fall.

Upon his old pine desk we drew
  His picture — pitiful to see,
Wrinkled and bald — half false, half true,
  And wrote beneath it, Twenty-three!

Next day came eight o'clock and nine,
  But *he* came not: our pulses quick
With play, we said it would be fine
  If the old Schoolmaster were sick.

And still the beech-trees bear the scars
  Of wounds which we that morning made,
Cutting their silvery bark to stars
  Whereon to count the games we played.

At last, as tired as we could be,
  Upon a clay-bank, strangely still,
We sat down in a row to see
  His worn-out hat come up the hill.

'T was hanging up at home — a quill
  Notched down, and sticking in the band,
And leaned against his arm-chair, still
  His staff was waiting for his hand.

Across his feet his threadbare coat
  Was lying, stuffed with many a roll
Of "copy-plates," and, sad to note,
  A dead rose in the button-hole.

And he no more might take his place
  Our lessons and our lives to plan:
Cold Death had kissed the wrinkled face
  Of that most gentle gentleman.

Ah me, what bitter tears made blind
  Our young eyes, for our thoughtless sin,
As two and two we walked behind
  The long black coffin he was in.

And all, sad women now, and men
  With wrinkles and gray hairs, can see
How he might wear a rose-bud then,
  And read love-verses tenderly.

THE best man should never pass by
  The worst, but to brotherhood true,
Entreat him thus gently, "Lo, I
  Am tempted in all things as you."

Of one dust all peoples are made,
  One sky doth above them extend,
And whether through sunshine or shade
  Their paths run, they meet at the end.

And whatever his honors may be, —
  Of riches, or genius, or blood,
God never made any man free
  To find out a separate good.

THE GRAY SWAN.

"Oh tell me, sailor, tell me true,
Is my little lad, my Elihu,
A-sailing with your ship?"
The sailor's eyes were dim with dew,—
"Your little lad, your Elihu?"
He said, with trembling lip,—
"What little lad? what ship?"

"What little lad! as if there could be
Another such an one as he!
What little lad, do you say?
Why, Elihu, that took to the sea
The moment I put him off my knee!
It was just the other day
The *Gray Swan* sailed away."

"The other day?" the sailor's eyes
Stood open with a great surprise, —
"The other day? the *Swan?*"
His heart began in his throat to rise.
"Ay, ay, sir, here in the cupboard lies
The jacket he had on."
"And so your lad is gone?"

"Gone with the *Swan.*" "And did she stand
With her anchor clutching hold of the sand,
For a month, and never stir?"
"Why, to be sure! I 've seen from the land,
Like a lover kissing his lady's hand,
The wild sea kissing her, —
A sight to remember, sir."

"But, my good mother, do you know
All this was twenty years ago?
I stood on the *Gray Swan's* deck,
And to that lad I saw you throw,
Taking it off, as it might be, so!
The kerchief from your neck."
"Ay, and he 'll bring it back!"

"And did the little lawless lad
That has made you sick and made you sad,
Sail with the *Gray Swan's* crew?"
"Lawless! the man is going mad!
The best boy ever mother had, —

Be sure he sailed with the crew!
What would you have him do?"

"And he has never written line,
Nor sent you word, nor made you sign
To say he was alive?"
"Hold! if 't was wrong, the wrong is mine;
Besides, he may be in the brine,
And could he write from the grave?
Tut, man! what would you have?"

"Gone twenty years, — a long, long cruise, —
'T was wicked thus your love to abuse;
But if the lad still live,
And come back home, think you you can
Forgive him?" — "Miserable man,
You 're mad as the sea, — you rave, —
What have I to forgive?"

The sailor twitched his shirt so blue,
And from within his bosom drew
The kerchief. She was wild.
"My God! my Father! is it true?
My little lad, my Elihu!
My blessed boy, my child!
My dead, my living child!"

THE WASHERWOMAN.

At the north end of our village stands,
With gable black and high,
A weather-beaten house, — I 've stopt
Often as I went by,

To see the strip of bleaching grass
Slipped brightly in between
The long straight rows of hollyhocks,
And current-bushes green;

The clumsy bench beside the door,
And oaken washing-tub,
Where poor old Rachel used to stand,
And rub, and rub, and rub!

Her blue-checked apron speckled with
The suds, so snowy white;
From morning when I went to school
Till I went home at night,

She never took her sunburnt arms
Out of the steaming tub:
We used to say 't was weary work
Only to hear her rub.

With sleeves stretched straight upon the grass
  The washed shirts used to lie;
By dozens I have counted them
  Some days, as I went by.

The burly blacksmith, battering at
  His red-hot iron bands,
Would make a joke of wishing that
  He had old Rachel's hands!

And when the sharp and ringing strokes
  Had doubled up his shoe,
As crooked as old Rachel's back,
  He used to say 't would do.

And every village housewife, with
  A conscience clear and light,
Would send for her to come and wash
  An hour or two at night!

Her hair beneath her cotton cap
  Grew silver-white and thin;
And the deep furrows in her face
  Ploughed all the roses in.

Yet patiently she kept at work, —
  We school-girls used to say
The smile about her sunken mouth
  Would quite go out some day.

Nobody ever thought the spark
  That in her sad eyes shone,
Burned outward from a living soul
  Immortal as their own.

And though a tender flush sometimes
  Into her cheek would start,
Nobody dreamed old Rachel had
  A woman's loving heart!

At last she left her heaps of clothes
  One quiet autumn day,
And stript from off her sunburnt arms
  The weary suds away;

That night within her moonlit door
  She sat alone, — her chin
Sunk in her hand, — her eyes shut up,
  As if to look within.

Her face uplifted to the star
  That stood so sweet and low
Against old crazy Peter's house —
  (He loved her long ago!)

Her heart had worn her body to
  A handful of poor dust, —
Her soul was gone to be arrayed
  In marriage-robes, I trust.

GROWING RICH.

AND why are you pale, my Nora?
  And why do you sigh and fret?
The black ewe had twin lambs to-day,
  And we shall be rich folk yet.

Do you mind the clover-ridge, Nora,
  That slopes to the crooked stream?
The brown cow pastured there this week,
  And her milk is sweet as cream.

The old gray mare that last year fell
  As thin as any ghost,
Is getting a new white coat, and looks
  As young as her colt, almost.

And if the corn-land should do well,
  And so, please God, it may,
I 'll buy the white-faced bull a bell,
  To make the meadows gay.

I know we are growing rich, Johnny,
  And that is why I fret,
For my little brother Phil is down
  In the dismal coal-pit yet.

And when the sunshine sets in th' corn,
  The tassels green and gay,
It will not touch my father's eyes,
  That are going blind, they say.

But if I were not sad for him,
  Nor yet for little Phil,
Why, darling Molly's hand, last year,
  Was cut off in the mill.

And so, nor mare nor brown milch-cow,
  Nor lambs can joy impart,
For the blind old man and th' mill and mine
  Are all upon my heart.

Too much of joy is sorrowful,
  So cares must needs abound;
The vine that bears too many flowers
  Will trail upon the ground.

SANDY MACLEOD.

WHEN I think of the weary nights and days
Of poor, hard-working folk, always
I see, with his head on his bosom bowed,
The luckless shoemaker, Sandy Macleod.

Jeering schoolboys used to say
His chimney would never be raked away
By the moon, and you by a jest so rough
May know that his cabin was low enough.

Nothing throve with him; his colt and cow
Got their living, he did n't know how, —
Yokes on their scraggy necks swinging about,
Beating and bruising them year in and out.

Out at the elbow he used to go, —
Alas for him that he did not know
The way to make poverty regal, — not he,
If such way under the sun there be.

Sundays all day in the door he sat,
A string of withered-up crape on his hat,
The crown half fallen against his head,
And half sewed in with a shoemaker's thread.

Sometimes with his hard and toil-worn hand
He would smooth and straighten th' faded band,
Thinking perhaps of a little mound
Black with nettles the long year round.

Blacksmith and carpenter, both were poor,
And there was the schoolmaster who, to be sure,
Had seen rough weather, but after all
When they met Sandy he went to the wall.

His wife was a lady, they used to say,
Repenting at leisure her wedding-day,
And that she was come of a race too proud
E'er to have mated with Sandy Macleod!

So fretting she sat from December to June,
While Sandy, poor soul, to a funeral-tune
Would beat out his hard, heavy leather, until
He set himself up, and got strength to be still.

It was not the full moon that made it so light
In the poor little dwelling of Sandy one night,
It was not the candles all shining around, —
Ah, no! 't was the light of the day he had found.

THE PICTURE-BOOK.

The black walnut-logs in the chimney
  Made ruddy the house with their light,
And the pool in the hollow was covered
  With ice like a lid, — it was night;

And Roslyn and I were together, —
  I know now the pleased look he wore,
And the shapes of the shadows that checkered
  The hard yellow planks of the floor;

And how, when the wind stirred the candle,
  Affrighted they ran from its gleams,
And crept up the wall to the ceiling
  Of cedar, and hid by the beams.

There were books on the mantel-shelf, dusty,
  And shut, and I see in my mind,
The pink-colored primer of pictures
  We stood on our tiptoes to find.

We opened the leaves where a camel
  Was seen on a sand-covered track,
A-snuffing for water, and bearing
  A great bag of gold on his back;

And talked of the free flowing rivers
  A tithe of his burden would buy,
And said, when the lips of the sunshine
  Had sucked his last water-skin dry;

With thick breath and mouth gaping open,
  And red eyes a-strain in his head,
His bones would push out as if buzzards
  Had picked him before he was dead!

Then turned the leaf over, and finding
  A palace that banners made gay,
Forgot the bright splendor of roses
  That shone through our windows in May;

And sighed for the great beds of princes,
  While pillows for him and for me
Lay soft among ripples of ruffles
  As sweet and as white as could be.

And sighed for their valleys, forgetting
  How warmly the morning sun kissed
Our hills, as they shrugged their green shoulders
  Above the white sheets of the mist.

Their carpets of dyed wool were softer,
  We said, than the planks of our floor,
Forgetting the flowers that in summer
  Spread out their gold mats at our door.

The storm spit its wrath in the chimney,
  And blew the cold ashes aside,
And only one poor little fagot
  Hung out its red tongue as it died,

When Roslyn and I through the darkness
  Crept off to our shivering beds,
A thousand vague fancies and wishes
  Still wildly astir in our heads:

Not guessing that we, too, were straying
  In thought on a sand-covered track,
Like the camel a-dying for water,
  And bearing the gold on his back.

He spoils his house and throws his pains away
  Who, as the sun veers, builds his windows o'er,
For, should he wait, the Light, some time of day,
  Would come and sit beside him in his door.

A WALK THROUGH THE SNOW.

I WALKED from our wild north country once,
  In a driving storm of snow;
Forty and seven miles in a day —
  You smile, — do you think it slow?
You would n't if ever you had ploughed
  Through a storm like that, I trow.

There was n't a cloud as big as my hand,
  The summer before, in the sky;
The grass in th' meadows was ground to dust,
  The springs and wells went dry;
We must have corn, and three stout men
  Were picked to go and buy.

Well, I was one; two bags I swung
  Across my shoulder, so!
And kissed my wife and boys, — their eyes
  Were blind to see me go.
'T was a bitter day, and just as th' sun
  Went down, we met the snow!

At first we whistled and laughed and sung,
  Our blood so nimbly stirred;
But as the snow-clogs dragged at our feet,
  And the air grew black and blurred,
We walked together for miles and miles,
  And did not speak a word!

I never saw a wilder storm:
  It blew and beat with a will;
Beside me, like two men of sleet,
  Walked my two mates, until
They fell asleep in their armor of ice,
  And both of them stood still.

I knew that they were warm enough,
  And yet I could not bear
To strip them of their cloaks; their eyes
  Were open and a-stare;
And so I laid their hands across
  Their breasts, and left them there.

And ran, — O Lord, I cannot tell
  How fast! in my dismay
I thought the fences and the trees —
  The cattle, where they lay
So black against their stacks of snow —
  All swam the other way!

And when at dawn I saw a hut,
  With smoke upcurling wide,
I thought it must have been my mates
  That lived, and I that died;
'T was heaven to see through th' frosty panes
  The warm, red cheeks inside!

THE glance that doth thy neighbor doubt
  Turn thou, O man, within,
And see if it will not bring out
  Some unsuspected sin.

To hide from shame the branded brow,
  Make broad thy charity,
And judge no man, except as thou
  Wouldst have him judge of thee.

THE WATER-BEARER.

'T WAS in the middle of summer,
  And burning hot the sun,
That Margaret sat on the low-roofed porch,
  A-singing as she spun:

Singing a ditty of slighted love,
  That shook with every note
The softly shining hair that fell
  In ripples round her throat.

The changeful color of her cheek
  At a breath would fall and rise,
And even th' sunny lights of hope
  Made shadows in her eyes.

Beneath the snowy petticoat
  You guessed the feet were bare,
By the slippers near her on the floor, —
  A dainty little pair.

She loved the low and tender tones
  The wearied summer yields,
When out of her wheaten leash she slips
  And strays into frosty fields.

And better than th' time that all
  The air with music fills,
She loved the little sheltered nest
  Alive with yellow bills.

But why delay my tale, to make
  A poem in her praise?
Enough that truth and virtue shone
  In all her modest ways.

'T was noon-day when the housewife said,
  "Now, Margaret, leave undone
Your task of spinning-work, and set
  Your wheel out of the sun;

"And tie your slippers on, and take
The cedar-pail with bands
Yellow as gold, and bear to the field
Cool water for the hands!"

And Margaret set her wheel aside,
And breaking off her thread,
Went forth into the harvest-field
With her pail upon her head, —

Her pail of sweetest cedar-wood,
With shining yellow bands,
Through clover reaching its red tops
Almost into her hands.

Her ditty flowing on the air,
For she did not break her song,
And the water dripping o'er th' grass,
From her pail as she went along, —

Over the grass that said to her,
Trembling through all its leaves,
"A bright rose for some harvester
To bind among his sheaves!"

And clouds of gay green grasshoppers
Flew up the way she went,
And beat their wings against their sides,
And chirped their discontent.

And the blackbird left the piping of
His amorous, airy glee,
And put his head beneath his wing, —
An evil sign to see.

The meadow-herbs, as if they felt
Some secret wound, in showers
Shook down their bright buds till her way
Was ankle-deep with flowers.

But Margaret never heard th' voice
That sighed in th' grassy leaves,
"A bright rose for some harvester
To bind among his sheaves!"

Nor saw the clouds of grasshoppers
Along her path arise,
Nor th' daisy hang her head aside
And shut her golden eyes.

She never saw the blackbird when
He hushed his amorous glee,
And put his head beneath his wing, —
That evil sign to see.

Nor did she know the meadow-herbs
Shook down their buds in showers
To choke her pathway, though her feet
Were ankle-deep in flowers.

But humming still of slighted love,
  That shook at every note
The softly shining hair that fell
  In ripples round her throat,

She came 'twixt winrows heaped as high,
  And higher than her waist,
And under a bush of sassafras
  The cedar-pail she placed.

And with the drops like starry rain
  A-glittering in her hair,
She gave to every harvester
  His cool and grateful share.

But there was one with eyes so sweet
  Beneath his shady brim,
That thrice within the cedar-pail
  She dipped her cup for him!

What wonder if a young man's heart
  Should feel her beauty's charm,
And in his fancy clasp her like
  The sheaf within his arm;

What wonder if his tender looks,
  That seemed the sweet disguise
Of sweeter things unsaid, should make
  A picture in her eyes!

What wonder if the single rose
  That graced her cheek erewhile,
Deepened its cloudy crimson, till
  It doubled in his smile!

Ah me! the housewife never said,
  Again, when Margaret spun, —
"Now leave your task awhile, and set
  Your wheel out of the sun;

"And tie your slippers on, and take
  The pail with yellow bands,
And bear into the harvest-field
  Cool water for the hands."

For every day, and twice a-day,
  Did Margaret break her thread,
And singing, hasten to the field,
  With her pail upon her head, —

Her pail of sweetest cedar-wood,
  And shining yellow bands, —
For all her care was now to bear
  Cool water to the hands.

What marvel if the young man's love
  Unfolded leaf by leaf,
Until within his arms ere long
  He clasped her like a sheaf!

What marvel if 't was Margaret's heart
  With fondest hopes that beat,
While th' young man's fancy idle lay
  As his sickle in the wheat.

That, while her thought flew, maiden-like.
  To years of marriage bliss,
His lay like a bee in a flower, shut up
  Within the moment's kiss!

What marvel if his love grew cold,
  And fell off leaf by leaf,
And that her heart was choked to death,
  Like the rose within his sheaf.

When autumn filled her lap with leaves,
  Yellow, and cold, and wet,
The bands of th' pail turned black, and th' wheel
  On the porch-side, idle set.

And Margaret's hair was combed and tied
  Under a cap of lace,
And th' housewife held the baby up
  To kiss her quiet face;

And all the sunburnt harvesters
  Stood round the door, — each one
Telling of some good word or deed
  That she had said or done.

Nay, there was one that pulled about
  His face his shady brim,
As if it were his kiss, not Death's,
  That made her eyes so dim.

And while the tearful women told
  That when they pinned her shroud,
One tress from th' ripples round her neck
  Was gone, he wept aloud;

And answered, pulling down his brim
  Until he could not see,
It was some ghost that stole the tress,
  For that it was not he!

'T is years since on the cedar-pail
  The yellow bands grew black, —
'T is years since in the harvest-field
  They turned th' green sod back

To give poor Margaret room, and all
  Who chance that way to pass,
May see at the head of her narrow bed
  A bush of sassafras.

Yet often in the time o' th' year
  When the hay is mown and spread,
There walks a maid in th' midnight shade
  With a pail upon her head.

THE BEST JUDGMENT.

Get up, my little handmaid,
  And see what you will see;
The stubble-fields and all the fields
  Are white as they can be.

Put on your crimson cashmere,
  And hood so soft and warm,
With all its woollen linings,
  And never heed the storm.

For you must find the miller
  In the west of Wertburg-town,
And bring me meal to feed my cows,
  Before the sun is down.

Then woke the little handmaid,
  From sleeping on her arm,
And took her crimson cashmere,
  And hood with woollen warm;

And bridle, with its buckles
  Of silver, from the wall,
And rode until the golden sun
  Was sloping to his fall.

Then on the miller's door-stone,
  In the west of Wertburg-town,
She dropt the bridle from her hands,
  And quietly slid down.

And when to her sweet face her beast
  Turned round, as if he said,
"How cold I am!" she took her hood
  And put it on his head.

Soft spoke she to the miller,
  "Nine cows are stalled at home,
And hither for three bags of meal,
  To feed them, I am come."

Now when the miller saw the price
  She brought was not by half
Enough to buy three bags of meal,
  He filled up two with chaff.

The night was wild and windy,
  The moon was thin and old,
As home the little handmaid rode,
  All shivering with the cold,

Beside the river, black with ice,
  And through the lonesome wood;
The snow upon her hair the while
  A-gathering like a hood.

And when beside the roof-tree
  Her good beast neighed aloud,
Her pretty crimson cashmere
  Was whiter than a shroud.

"Get down, you silly handmaid,"
  The old dame cried, "get down, —
You 've been a long time riding
  From the west of Wertburg-town!"

And from her oaken settle
  Forth hobbled she amain, —
Alas! the slender little hands
  Were frozen to the rein.

Then came the neighbors, one and all,
  With melancholy brows,
Mourning because the dame had lost
  The keeper of her cows.

And cursing the rich miller,
  In blind, misguided zeal,
Because he sent two bags of chaff
  And only one of meal.

Dear Lord, how little man's award
  The right or wrong attest,
And he who judges least, I think,
  Is he who judges best.

HUGH THORNDYKE.

EGALTON'S hills are sunny,
  And brave with oak and pine,
And Egalton's sons and daughters
  Are tall and straight and fine.

The harvests in the summer
  Cover the land like a smile,
For Egalton's men and women
  Are busy all the while.

'T is merry in the mowing
  To see the great swath fall,
And the little laughing maidens
  Raking, one and all.

Their heads like golden lilies
  Shining over the hay,
And every one among them
  As sweet as a rose in May.

And yet despite the favor
  Which Heaven doth thus allot,
Egalton has its goblin,
  As what good land has not?

Hugh Thorndyke — (peace be with him,
He is not living now) —
Was tempted by this creature
One day to leave his plow,

And sit beside the furrow
In a shadow cool and sweet,
For the lying goblin told him
That *he* would sow his wheat.

And told him this, moreover,
That if he would not mind,
His house should burn to ashes,
His children be struck blind!

So, trusting half, half frightened,
Poor Hugh with many a groan
Waited beside the furrow,
But the wheat was never sown.

And when the fields about him
Grew white, — with very shame
He told his story, giving
The goblin all the blame.

Now Hugh's wife loved her husband,
And when he told her this,
She took his brawny hands in hers
And gave them each a kiss,

Saying, we ourselves this goblin
  Shall straightway lay to rest, —
The more he does his worst, dear Hugh,
  The more we 'll do our best!

To work they went, and all turned out
  Just as the good wife said,
And Hugh was blest,— his corn that year,
  Grew higher than his head.

They sing a song in Egalton
  Hugh made there, long ago,
Which says that honest love and work
  Are all we need below.

STILL from the unsatisfying quest
  To know the final plan,
I turn my soul to what is best
  In nature and in man.

FAITHLESS.

SEVEN great windows looking seaward,
  Seven smooth columns white and high;
Here it was we made our bright plans,
  Mildred Jocelyn and I.

Soft and sweet the water murmured
  By yon stone wall, low and gray,
'T was the moonlight and the midnight
  Of the middle of the May.

On the porch, now dark and lonesome,
  Sat we as the hours went by,
Fearing nothing, hoping all things,
  Mildred Jocelyn and I.

Singing low and pleasant ditties,
  Kept the tireless wind his way,
Through the moonlight and the midnight,
  Of the middle of the May.

Not for sake of pleasant ditties,
  Such as winds may sing or sigh,
Sat we on the porch together,
  Mildred Jocelyn and I.

Shrilly crew the cock so watchful,
  Answering to the watch-dog's bay,
In the moonlight and the midnight
  Of the middle of the May.

Had the gates of Heaven been open
  We would then have passed them by,
Well content with earthly pleasures,
  Mildred Jocelyn and I.

I have seen the bees thick-flying, —
  Azure-winged and ringed with gold;
I have seen the sheep from washing
  Come back snowy to the fold;

And her hair was bright as bees are,
  Bees with shining golden bands;
And no wool was ever whiter
  Than her little dimpled hands.

Oft we promised to be lovers,
  Howe'er fate our faith should try;
Giving kisses back for kisses,
  Mildred Jocelyn and I.

Tears, sad tears, be stayed from falling;
  Ye can bring no faintest ray
From the moonlight and the midnight
  Of the middle of the May.

If some friend would come and tell me,
  "On your Mildred's eyes so blue
Grass has grown, but on her death-bed
  She was saying prayers for you;"

Here beside the smooth white columns
  I should not so grieve to-day,
For the moonlight and the midnight
  Of the middle of the May.

Do not look for wrong and evil —
  You will find them if you do;
As you measure for your neighbor
  He will measure back to you.

Look for goodness, look for gladness,
  You will meet them all the while;
If you bring a smiling visage
  To the glass, you meet a smile.

MY FADED SHAWL.

TELL you a story, do you
say?
Whatever my wits re-
member?
Well, going down to the
woods one day
Through the winds o'
the wild November,
I met a lad, called Char-
ley.

We lived on the crest o' the Krumley
ridge,
And I was a farmer's daughter,
And under the hill by the Krumley bridge
Of the crazy Krumley water,
Lived this poor lad, Charley.

Right well I knew his ruddy cheek,
And step as light as a feather,
Although we never were used to speak,
And never to play together,
I and this poor lad Charley.

So, when I saw him hurrying down
  My path, will you believe me?
I knit my brow to an ugly frown, —
  Forgive me, O forgive me!
    Sweet shade of little Charley.

The dull clouds dropped their skirts of snow
  On the hills, and made them colder;
I was only twelve years old, or so,
  And may be a twelvemonth older
    Was Charley, dearest Charley.

A faded shawl, with flowers o' blue,
  All tenderly and fairly
Enwrought by his mother's hand, I knew,
  He wore that day, my Charley,
    My little love, my Charley.

His great glad eyes with light were lit
  Like the dewy light o' the morning;
His homespun jacket, not a whit
  Less proudly, for my scorning,
    He wore, brave-hearted Charley.

I bore a pitcher, — 't was our pride, —
  At the fair my father won it,
And consciously I turned the side
  With the golden lilies on it,
    To dazzle the eyes o' Charley.

This pitcher, and a milk-white loaf,
  Piping hot from the platter,
When, where the path turned sharply off
  To the crazy Krumley water,
    I came upon my Charley.

He smiled, — my pulses never stirred
  From their still and steady measures,
Till the wind came flapping down like a bird
  And caught away my treasures.
    "Help me, O Charley! Charley!

My loaf, my golden lilies gone!"
  My heart was all a-flutter;
For I saw them whirling on and on
  To the frozen Krumley water,
    And then I saw my Charley,

The frayed and faded shawl from his neck
  Unknot, with a quick, wise cunning,
And speckled with snow-flakes, toss it back,
  That he might be free for running.
    My good, great-hearted Charley.

I laid it softly on my arm,
  I warmed it in my bosom,
And traced each broider-stitch to the form
  Of its wilding model blossom,
    For sake of my gentle Charley.

Away, away! like a shadow fleet!
  The air was thick and blinding;
The icy stones were under his feet,
  And the way was steep and winding.
      Come back! come back, my Charley!

He waved his ragged cap in the air,
  My childish fears to scatter;
Dear Lord, was it Charley? Was he there,
  On th' treacherous crust o' th' water?
      No more! 't is death! my Charley.

The thin blue glittering sheet of ice
  Bends, breaks, and falls asunder;
His arms are lifted once, and twice!
  My God! he is going under!
      He is drowned! he is dead! my Charley.

The wild call stops, — the blood runs chill;
  I dash the tears from my lashes,
And strain my gaze to th' foot o' th' hill, —
  Who flies so fast through the rushes?
      My drownèd love? my Charley?

My brain is wild, — I laugh, I cry, —
  The chill blood thaws and rallies;
What holds he thus, so safe and high?
  My loaf? and my golden lilies?
      Charley! my sweet, sweet Charley!

Across my mad brain word on word
  Of tenderness went whirling;
I kissed him, called him my little bird
  O' th' woods, my dove, my darling, —
    My true, true love, my Charley.

In what sweet phrases he replied
  I know not now — no matter —
This only, that he would have died
  In the crazy Krumley water
    To win my praise, — dear Charley!

He took the frayed and faded shawl,
  For his sake warmed all over,
And wrapped me round and round with all
  The tenderness of a lover, —
    My best, my bravest Charley!

And when his shoes o' the snows were full, —
  Ay, full to their tops, — a-smiling
He said they were lined with a fleece o' wool,
  The pain o' th' frost beguiling.
    Was ever a lad like Charley?

So down the slope o' th' Krumley ridge,
  Our hands locked fast together,
And over the crazy Krumley bridge,
  We went through the freezing weather, —
    I and my drownèd Charley.

The cornfields all of ears were bare;
  But the stalks, so bright and brittle,
And the black and empty husks were there
  For the mouths of the hungry cattle.
    We passed them, I and Charley,

And passed the willow-tree that went
  With the wind, as light as a feather,
And th' two proud oaks with their shoulders bent
  Till their faces came together, —
    Whispering, I said to Charley:

The hollow sycamore, so white,
  The old gum, straight and solemn,
With never the curve of a root in sight;
  But set in the ground like a column, —
    I, prattling to my Charley.

We left behind the sumach hedge,
  And the waste of stubble crossing,
Came at last to the dusky edge
  Of the woods, so wildly tossing, —
    I and my quiet Charley.

Ankle-deep in the leaves we stood, —
  The leaves that were brown as leather,
And saw the choppers chopping the wood, —
  Seven rough men together, —
    I and my drooping Charley.

I see him now as I saw him stand
  With my loaf — he had hardly won it —
And the beautiful pitcher in his hand,
  With the golden lilies on it, —
    My little saint, — my Charley.

The stubs were burning here and there,
  The winds the fierce flames blowing,
And the arms o' th' choppers, brown and bare,
  Now up, now down are going, —
    I turn to them from Charley.

Right merrily the echoes ring
  From the sturdy work a-doing,
And as the woodsmen chop, they sing
  Of the girls that they are wooing.
    O what a song for Charley!

This way an elm begins to lop,
  And that, its balance losing,
And the squirrel comes from his nest in the top,
  And sits in the boughs a-musing.
    What ails my little Charley?

The loaf from out his hand he drops,
  His eyelid flutters, closes;
He tries to speak, he whispers, stops, —
  His mouth its rose-red loses, —
    One look, just one, my Charley!

And now his white and frozen cheek
  Each wild-eyed chopper fixes,
And never a man is heard to speak
  As they set their steel-blue axes,
    And haste to the help o' Charley!

Say, what does your beautiful pitcher hold?
  Come tell us if you can, sir!
The chopper's question was loud and bold,
  But never a sign nor answer:
    All fast asleep was Charley.

The stubs are burning low to th' earth,
  The winds the fierce flames flaring,
And now to the edge of the crystal hearth
  The men in their arms are bearing
    The clay-cold body of Charley.

O'er heart, o'er temple those rude hands go,
  Each hand as light as a brother's,
As they gather about him in the snow,
  Like a company of mothers, —
    My dead, my darling Charley.

Before them all, (my heart grew bold,)
  From off my trembling bosom,
I unwound the mantle, fold by fold,
  All for my blighted blossom,
    My sweet white flower, — my Charley.

I have tokens large, I have tokens small
  Of all my life's lost pleasures,
But that poor frayed and faded shawl
  Is the treasure of my treasures, —
    The first, last gift of Charley.

CARE.

Care is like a husbandman
  Who doth guard our treasures.
And the while, all ways he can,
  Spoils our harmless pleasures.

Loving hearts and laughing brows,
  Most he seeks to plunder,
And each furrow that he ploughs
  Turns the roses under.

OLD CHUMS.

Is it you, Jack? Old boy, is it really you?
I should n't have known you but that I was told
You might be expected; — pray, how do you do?
But what, under heaven, has made you so old?

Your hair! why, you 've only a little gray fuzz!
And your beard 's white! but that can be beautifully dyed;
And your legs are n't but just half as long as they was;
And then — stars and garters! your vest is so wide!

Is this your hand? Lord, how I envied you that
In the time of our courting, — so soft, and so small,
And now it is callous inside, and so fat, —
Well, you beat the very old deuce, that is all.

Turn round! let me look at you! is n't it odd,
How strange in a few years a fellow's chum grows!
Your eye is shrunk up like a bean in a pod,
And what are these lines branching out from your nose?

Your back has gone up and your shoulders gone down,
  And all the old roses are under the plough;
Why, Jack, if we 'd happened to meet about town,
  I would n't have known you from Adam, I vow!

You 've had trouble, have you? I 'm sorry; but, John,
  All trouble sits lightly at your time of life.
How 's Billy, my namesake? You don't say he 's gone
  To the war, John, and that you have buried your
    wife?

Poor Katharine! so she has left you — ah me!
  I thought she would live to be fifty, or more.
What is it you tell me? She *was* fifty-three!
  O no, Jack! she was n't so much, by a score!

Well, there 's little Katy, — was that her name, John?
  She 'll rule your house one of these days like a queen.
That baby! good Lord! is she married and gone?
  With a Jack ten years old! and a Katy fourteen!

Then I give it up! Why, you 're younger than I
  By ten or twelve years, and to think you 've come
    back
A sober old graybeard, just ready to die!
  I don't understand how it is — do you, Jack?

I 've got all my faculties yet, sound and bright;
  Slight failure my eyes are beginning to hint;

But still, with my spectacles on, and a light
 'Twixt them and the page, I can read any print.

My hearing *is* dull, and my leg is more spare,
 Perhaps, than it was when I beat you at ball;
My breath gives out, too, if I go up a stair, —
 But nothing worth mentioning, nothing at all!

My hair is just turning a little, you see,
 And lately I 've put on a broader-brimmed hat
Than I wore at your wedding, but you will agree,
 Old fellow, I look all the better for that.

I 'm sometimes a little rheumatic, 't is true,
 And my nose is n't quite on a straight line, they say;
For all that, I don't think I 've changed much, do you?
 And I don't feel a day older, Jack, not a day.

APART from the woes that are dead and gone,
 And the shadow of future care,
The heaviest yoke of the present hour
 Is easy enough to bear.

THE SHOEMAKER.

Now the hickory with its hum
  Cheers the wild and rainy weather,
And the shoemaker has come
  With his lapstone, last, and leather.

With his head as white as wool,
  With the wrinkles getting bolder,
And his heart with news as full
  As the wallet on his shoulder.

How the children's hearts will beat,
  How their eyes will shine with pleasure
As he sets their little feet,
  Bare and rosy, in his measure.

And how, behind his chair,
  They will steal grave looks to summon,
As he ties away his hair
  From his forehead, like a woman.

When he tells the merry news
  How their eyes will laugh and glisten,
While the mother binds the shoes
  And they gather round and listen.

But each one, leaning low
  On his lapstone, will be crying,
As he tells how little Jo,
  With a broken back, is dying.

Of the way he came to fall
  In the flowery April weather,
Of the new shoes on the wall
  That are hanging, tied together.

How the face of little Jo
  Has grown white, and they who love him
See the shadows come and go,
  As if angels flew above him.

And the old shoemaker, true
  To the woe of the disaster,
Will uplift his apron blue
  To his eyes, then work the faster.

TO THE WIND.

Steer hither, rough old mariner,
  Keeping your jolly crew
Beating about in the seas of life, —
  Steer hither, and tell me true
About my little son, Maximus,
  Who sailed away with you!

Seven and twenty years ago
  He came to us, — ah me!
The snow that fell that whistling night
  Was not so pure as he,
And I was rich enough, I trow,
  When I took him on my knee.

I was rich enough, and when I met
  A man, unthrift and lorn,
Whom I a hundred times had met
  With less of pity than scorn,
I opened my purse, — it was well for him
  That Maximus was born!

We have five boys at home, erect
  And straight of limb, and tall,
Gentle, and loving all that God
  Has made, or great or small,
But Maximus, our youngest born,
  Was the gentlest of them all!

Yet was he brave, — they all are brave,
  Not one for favor or frown
That fears to set his strength against
  The bravest of the town,
But this, our little Maximus,
  Could fight when he was down.

Six darling boys! not one of all,
  If we had had to choose,
Could we have singled from the rest
  To sail on such a cruise,
But surely little Maximus
  Was not the one to lose!

His hair divided into slips,
  And tumbled every way, —
His mother always called them curls,
  She has one to this day, —
And th' nails of his hands were thin and red
  As the leaves of a rose in May.

Steer hither, rough mariner, and bring
  Some news of our little lad, —
If he be anywhere out of th' grave
  It will make his mother glad,
Tho' he grieved her more with his waywardness
  Than all the boys she had.

I know it was against himself,
  For he was good and kind,
That he left us, though he saw our eyes
  With tears, for his sake, blind, —
O how can you give to such as he,
  Your nature, wilful wind!

WHAT comfort, when with clouds of woe
  The heart is burdened, and must weep,
To feel that pain must end, — to know,
  "He giveth his beloved sleep."

When in the mid-day march we meet
  The outstretched shadows of the night,
The promise, how divinely sweet,
  "At even-time it shall be light."

LITTLE CYRUS.

Emily Mayfield all the day
  Sits and rocks her cradle alone,
And never a neighbor comes to say
  How pretty little Cyrus has grown.

Meekly Emily's head is hung,
  Many a sigh from her bosom breaks,
And ne'er such pitiful tune was sung
  As that her lowly lullaby makes.

Near where the village schoolhouse stands.
  On the grass by the mossy spring,
Merry children are linking hands,
  But little Cyrus is not in the ring.

"They might make room for me, if they tried,'
  He thinks as he listens to call and shout,
And his eyes so pretty are open wide,
  Wondering why they have left him out.

Nightly hurrying home they go,
  Each, of the praise he has had, to boast
But never an honor can Cyrus show,
  And yet he studies his book the most.

Little Cyrus is out in the hay, —
  Not where the clover is sweet and red,
With mates of his tender years at play,
  But where the stubble is sharp, instead,

And every flowerless shrub and tree
  That takes the twinkling noontide heat,
Is dry and dusty as it can be;
  There with his tired, sunburnt feet

Dragging wearily, Cyrus goes,
  Trying to sing as the others do,
But never the stoutest hand that mows
  Says, "It is work too hard for you,

Little Cyrus, your hands so small
  Bleed with straining to keep your place,
And the look that says I must bear it all
  Is sadder than tears in your childish face:

So give me your knotty swath to mow,
  And rest awhile on the shady sward,
Else your body will crooked grow,
  Little Cyrus, from working hard."

If he could listen to words like that,
  The stubble would not be half so rough
To his naked feet, and his ragged hat
  Would shield him from sunshine well enough.

But ne'er a moment the mowers check
  Song or whistle, to think of him,
With blisters burning over his neck,
  Under his straw hat's ragged brim.

So, stooping over the field he goes,
  With none to pity if he complain,
And so the crook in his body grows,
  And he never can stand up straight again.

The cattle lie down in the lane so still, —
  The scythes in the apple-tree shine bright,
And Cyrus sits on the ashen sill
  Watching the motes, in the streaks of light,

Quietly slanting out of the sky,
  Over the hill to the porch so low,
Wondering if in the world on high
  There will be any briery fields to mow.

Emily Mayfield, pale and weak,
  Steals to his side in the light so dim,
And the single rose in his swarthy cheek
  Grows double, the while she says to him, —

Little Cyrus, 't is many a day
  Since one with just your own sweet eyes,
And a voice as rich as a bird's in May,
  (Gently she kisses the boy and sighs,)

Here on the porch when the work was done,
  Sat with a young girl, (not like me,)
Her heart was light as the wool she spun,
  And her laughter merry as it could be;

Her hair was silken, he used to say,
  When they sat on the porch-side, "woful when,'
And I know the clover you mowed to-day
  Was not more red than her cheeks were then.

He told her many a story wild,
  Like this, perhaps, which I tell to you,
And she was a woman less than child,
  And thought whatever he said was true.

From home and kindred, — ah me, ah me!
  With only her faith in his love, she fled,
'T was all like a dreaming, and when she could see
  She owned she was sinful and prayed to be dead.

But always, however long she may live,
  Desolate, desolate, she shall repine,
And so with no love to receive or to give,
  Her face is as sad and as wrinkled as mine.

Little Cyrus, trembling, lays
  His head on his mother's knee to cry,
And kissing his sunburnt cheek, she says,
  "Hush, my darling, it was not I."

Our God is love, and that which we miscall
  Evil, in this good world that He has made,
  Is meant to be a little tender shade
Between us and His glory, — that is all;
And he who loves the best his fellow man
Is loving God, the holiest way he can.

MORNING.

WAKE, Dillie, my darling, and kiss me,
  The daybreak is nigh, —
I can see, through the half-open curtain,
  A strip of blue sky.

Yon lake, in her valley-bed lying,
  Looks fair as a bride,
And pushes, to greet the sun's coming,
  The mist sheets aside.

The birds, to the wood-temple flying,
  Their matins to chant,
Are chirping their love to each other,
  With wings dropt aslant.

Not a tree, that the morning's bright edges
  With silver illumes,
But trembles and stirs with its pleasure
  Through all its green plumes.

Wake, Dillie, and join in the praises
  All nature doth give;
Clap hands, and rejoice in the goodness
  That leaves you to live.

For what is the world in her glory
  To that which thou art?
Thank God for the soul that is in you, —
  Thank God for your heart!

The world that had never a lover
  Her bright face to kiss, —
With her splendors of stars and of noontides
  How poor is her bliss!

Wake, Dillie, — the white vest of morning
  With crimson is laced;
And why should delights of God's giving
  Be running to waste!

Full measures, pressed down, are awaiting
  Our provident use;
And is there no sin in neglecting
  As well as abuse?

The cornstalk exults in its tassel,
  The flint in its spark, —
And shall the seed planted within me
  Rot out in the dark?

Shall I be ashamed to give culture
  To what God has sown?
When nature asks bread, shall I offer
  A serpent, or stone?

For could I out-weary its yearnings
  By fasting, or pain, —
Would life have a better fulfilment,
  Or death have a gain?

Nay, God will not leave us unanswered
  In any true need;
His will may be writ in an instinct,
  As well as a creed.

And, Dillie, my darling, believe me,
  That life is the best,
That, loving here, truly and sweetly,
  With Him leaves the rest.

Its head to the sweep of the whirlwind
  The wise willow suits, —
While the oak, that 's too stubborn for bending,
  Comes up by the roots.

Such lessons, each day, round about us,
  Our good Mother writes, —
To show us that Nature, in some way,
  Avenges her slights.

THE SUMMER STORM.

At noon-time I stood in the door-way to see
The spots, burnt like blisters, as white as could be.
Along the near meadow, shoved in like a wedge
Betwixt the high-road, and the stubble-land's edge.

The leaves of the elm-tree were dusty and brown,
The birds sat with shut eyes and wings hanging down
The corn reached its blades out, as if in the pain
Of crisping and scorching it felt for the rain.

Their meek faces turning away from the sun,
The cows waded up to their flanks in the run,
The sheep, so herd-loving, divided their flocks,
And singly lay down by the sides of the rocks.

At sunset there rose and stood black in the east
A cloud with the forehead and horns of a beast,
That quick to the zenith went higher and higher,
With feet that were thunder and eyes that were fire.

Then came a hot sough, like a gust of his breath,
And the leaves took the tremble and whiteness of death,—
The dog, to his master, from kennel and kin,
Came whining and shaking, with back crouching in.

At twilight the darkness was fearful to see:
"Make room," cried the children, "O mother, for me!"
As climbing her chair and her lap, with alarm,
And whisper, — "Was ever there seen such a storm!"

At morning, the run where the cows cooled their flanks
Had washed up a hedge of white roots from its banks;
The turnpike was left a blue streak, and each side
The gutters like rivers ran muddy and wide.

The barefooted lad started merry to school,
And the way was the nearest that led through the pool;
The red-bird wore never so shining a coat,
Nor the pigeon so glossy a ring on her throat.

The teamster sat straight in his place, for the nonce,
And sang to his sweetheart and team, both at once;
And neighbors shook hands o'er the fences that day,
And talked of their homesteads instead of their hay.

IF AND IF.

If I were a painter, I could paint
  The dwarfed and straggling wood,
And the hillside where the meeting-house
  With the wooden belfry stood,
A dozen steps from the door, — alone,
On four square pillars of rough gray stone.

We schoolboys used to write our names
  With our finger-tips each day
In th' dust o' th' cross-beams, — once it shone,
  I have heard the old folks say,
(Praising the time past, as old folks will,)
Like a pillar o' fire on the side o' th' hill.

I could paint the lonesome lime-kilns,
  And the lime-burners, wild and proud,
Their red sleeves gleaming in the smoke
  Like a rainbow in a cloud, —
Their huts by the brook, and their mimicking crew —
Making believe to be lime-burners too!

I could paint the brawny wood-cutter,
  With the patches at his knees, —
He 's been asleep these twenty years,
  Among his friends, the trees:
The day that he died, the best oak o' the wood
Came up by the roots, and he lies where it stood.

I could paint the blacksmith's dingy shop, —
  Its sign, a pillar of smoke;
The farm-horse halt, the rough-haired colt,
  And the jade with her neck in a yoke;
The pony that made to himself a law,
And would n't go under the saddle, nor draw!

The poor old mare at the door-post,
  With joints as stiff as its pegs, —
Her one white eye, and her neck awry, —
  Trembling the flies from her legs,
And the thriftless farmer that used to stand
And curry her ribs with a kindly hand.

I could paint his quaint old-fashioned house,
  With its windows, square and small,
And the seams of clay running every way
  Between the stones o' the wall:
The roof, with furrows of mosses green,
And new bright shingles set between.

The oven, bulging big behind,
  And the narrow porch before,
And the weather-cock for ornament
  On the pole beside the door;
And th' row of milk-pans, shining bright
As silver, in the summer light.

And I could paint his girls and boys,
  Each and every one,
Hepzibah sweet, with her little bare feet,
  And Shubal, the stalwart son,
And wife and mother, with home-spun gown,
And roses beginning to shade into brown.

I could paint the garden, with its paths
  Cut smooth, and running straight, —
The gray sage bed, the poppies red,
  And the lady-grass at the gate, —
The black warped slab with its hive of bees.
In the corner, under the apple-trees.

I could paint the fields, in the middle hush
  Of winter, bleak and bare,
Some snow like a lamb that is caught in a bush,
  Hanging here and there, —
The mildewed haystacks, all a-lop,
And the old dead stub with the crow at the top.

The cow, with a board across her eyes,
  And her udder dry as dust,
Her hide so brown, her horn turned down,
  And her nose the color of rust, —
The walnut-tree so stiff and high,
With its black bark twisted all awry.

The hillside, and the small space set
  With broken palings round, —
The long loose grass, and the little grave
  With the head-stone on the ground,
And the willow, like the spirit of grace
Bending tenderly over the place.

The miller's face, half smile, half frown,
  Were a picture I could paint,
And the mill, with gable steep and brown,
  And dripping wheel aslant, —
The weather-beaten door, set wide,
And the heaps of meal-bags either side.

The timbers cracked to gaping seams,
  The swallows' clay-built nests,
And the rows of doves that sit on the beams
  With plump and glossy breasts, —
The bear by his post sitting upright to eat,
With half of his clumsy legs in his feet.

I could paint the mill-stream, cut in two
  By the heat o' the summer skies,
And the sand-bar, with its long brown back,
  And round and bubbly eyes,
And the bridge, that hung so high o'er the tide,
Creaking and swinging from side to side.

The miller's pretty little wife,
  In the cottage that she loves, —
Her hand so white, and her step so light,
  And her eyes as brown as th' dove's,
Her tiny waist, and belt of blue,
And her hair that almost dazzles you.

I could paint the White-Hawk tavern, flanked
  With broken and wind-warped sheds,
And the rock where the black clouds used to sit,
  And trim their watery heads
With little sprinkles of shining light,
Night and morning, morning and night.

The road, where slow and wearily,
  The dusty teamster came, —
The sign on its post and the round-faced host,
  And the high arched door, aflame
With trumpet-flowers, — the well-sweep, high,
And the flowing water-trough, close by.

If I were a painter, and if my hand
  Were cunning, as it is not,
I could paint you a picture that would stand
  When all the rest were forgot;
But why should I tell you what it would be?
I never shall paint it, nor you ever see.

We are the mariners, and God the Sea,
  And though we make false reckonings, and run
Wide of a righteous course, and are undone,
  Out of his deeps of love, we cannot be.

For by those heavy strokes we misname ill,
  Through the fierce fire of sin, through tempering doubt,
Our natures more and more are beaten out
  To perfecter reflections of His will!

AN ORDER FOR A PICTURE.

O GOOD painter, tell me true,
  Has your hand the cunning to draw
  Shapes of things that you never saw?
Ay? Well, here is an order for you.

Woods and cornfields, a little brown, —
  The picture must not be over-bright, —
  Yet all in the golden and gracious light
Of a cloud, when the summer sun is down.
  Alway and alway, night and morn,
  Woods upon woods, with fields of corn
    Lying between them, not quite sere,
And not in the full, thick, leafy bloom,
When the wind can hardly find breathing-room
    Under their tassels, — cattle near,
Biting shorter the short green grass,
And a hedge of sumach and sassafras,

With bluebirds twittering all around, —
(Ah, good painter, you can't paint sound!) —
These, and the house where I was born,
Low and little, and black and old,
With children, many as it can hold,
All at the windows, open wide, —
Heads and shoulders clear outside,
And fair young faces all ablush:
Perhaps you may have seen, some day,
Roses crowding the self-same way,
Out of a wilding, wayside bush.

Listen closer. When you have done
With woods and cornfields and grazing herds,
A lady, the loveliest ever the sun
Looked down upon you must paint for me:
Oh, if I only could make you see
The clear blue eyes, the tender smile,
The sovereign sweetness, the gentle grace,
The woman's soul, and the angel's face
That are beaming on me all the while,
I need not speak these foolish words:
Yet one word tells you all I would say, —
She is my mother: you will agree
That all the rest may be thrown away.

Two little urchins at her knee
You must paint, sir: one like me, —
The other with a clearer brow,

And the light of his adventurous eyes
Flashing with boldest enterprise:
At ten years old he went to sea, —
God knoweth if he be living now, —
He sailed in the good ship "Commodore," —
Nobody ever crossed her track
To bring us news, and she never came back.
Ah, 't is twenty long years and more
Since that old ship went out of the bay
With my great-hearted brother on her deck:
I watched him till he shrank to a speck,
And his face was toward me all the way.
Bright his hair was, a golden brown,
The time we stood at our mother's knee:
That beauteous head, if it did go down,
Carried sunshine into the sea!

Out in the fields one summer night
We were together, half afraid
Of the corn-leaves' rustling, and of the shade
Of the high hills, stretching so still and far, —
Loitering till after the low little light
Of the candle shone through the open door,
And over the hay-stack's pointed top,
All of a tremble and ready to drop,
The first half-hour, the great yellow star,
That we, with staring, ignorant eyes,
Had often and often watched to see
Propped and held in its place in the skies

By the fork of a tall red mulberry-tree,
  Which close in the edge of our flax-field grew,—
Dead at the top,—just one branch full
Of leaves, notched round, and lined with wool,
  From which it tenderly shook the dew
Over our heads, when we came to play
In its handbreadth of shadow, day after day.
  Afraid to go home, Sir; for one of us bore
A nest full of speckled and thin-shelled eggs,—
The other, a bird, held fast by the legs,
Not so big as a straw of wheat:
The berries we gave her she would n't eat,
But cried and cried, till we held her bill,
So slim and shining, to keep her still.

At last we stood at our mother's knee.
  Do you think, Sir, if you try,
  You can paint the look of a lie?
  If you can, pray have the grace
  To put it solely in the face
Of the urchin that is likest me:
    I think 't was solely mine, indeed:
  But that's no matter,—paint it so;
    The eyes of our mother—(take good heed)—
Looking not on the nest-full of eggs,
Nor the fluttering bird, held so fast by the legs,
But straight through our faces down to our lies,
And, oh, with such injured, reproachful surprise!
  I felt my heart bleed where that glance went, as though
  A sharp blade struck through it.

You, Sir, know
That you on the canvas are to repeat
Things that are fairest, things most sweet,—
Woods and cornfields and mulberry-tree,—
The mother,—the lads, with their bird, at her knee:
But, oh, that look of reproachful woe!
High as the heavens your name I'll shout,
If you paint me the picture, and leave that out.

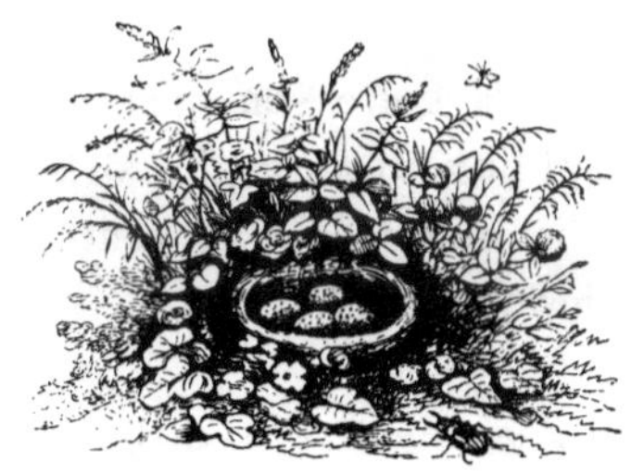

FIFTEEN AND FIFTY.

COME, darling, put your frown aside!
 I own my fault, 't is true, 't is true,
There is one picture that I hide,
 Even away from you!

Why, then, I do not love you? Nay,
 You wrong me there, my pretty one:
Remember you are in your May;
 My Summer days are done.

My autumn days are come, in truth,
 And blighting frosts begin to fall;
You are the sunny light of youth,
 That glorifies it all.

Even when winter clouds shall break
 In storms, I shall not mind, my dear,
For you within my heart shall make
 The springtime of the year!

In short, life did its best for me,
 When first our paths together ran;
But I had lived, you will agree,
 One life, ere yours began.

I must have smiled, I must have wept,
  Ere mirth or moan could do you wrong;
But come, and see the picture, kept
  Hidden away so long!

The walk will not be strange nor far, —
  Across the meadow, toward the tree
From whose thick top one silver star
  Uplifting slow, you see.

So, darling, we have gained the height
  Where lights and shadows softly meet;
Rest you a moment, — full in sight,
  My picture lies complete.

A hill-side dark, with woods behind,
  A strip of emerald grass before, —
A homely house ; some trees that blind
  Window, and wall, and door.

A singing streamlet, — either side
  Bordered with flowers, — geraniums gay,
And pinks, with red mouths open wide
  For sunshine, all the day.

A tasselled cornfield on one hand,
  And on the other, meadows green,
With angles of bright harvest bend
  Wedged sunnily between.

A world of smiling ways and walks,
  The hop-vines twisting through the pales,
The crimson cups o' the hollyhocks,
  The lilies, in white veils;

The porch with morning-glories gay,
  And sunken step, the well-sweep tall,
The barn, with roof 'twixt black and gray,
  And warpt, wind-shaken wall;

The garden with the fence of stone,
  The lane so dusky at the close,
The door-yard gate all overgrown
  With one wild smothering rose;

The honeysuckle that has blown
  His trumpet till his throat is red,
And the wild swallow, mateless flown
  Under the lonesome shed;

The corn, with bean-pods showing through,
  The fields that to the sunset lean,
The crooked paths along the dew,
  Telling of flocks unseen.

The bird in scarlet-colored coat
  Flying about the apple-tree;
The new moon in her shallow boat,
  Sailing alone, you see;

The aspen at the window-pane, —
  The pair of bluebirds on the peach, —
The yellow waves of ripening grain, —
  You see them all and each.

The shadows stretching to the door,
  From far-off hills, and nearer trees,
I cannot show you any more, —
  The landscape holds but these.

And yet, my darling, after all,
  'T is not *my* picture you behold;
Your house is ruined near to fall, —
  Your flowers are dew and mould.

I wish that you could only see,
  While the glad garden shines its best,
The little rose that was to me
  The queen of all the rest.

The bluebirds, — he with scarlet wings, —
  The silver brook, the sunset glow,
To me are but the signs of things
  The landscape cannot show.

That old house was our home — not *ours!*
  You were not born — how could it be?
That window where you see the flowers,
  Is where she watched for me,

So pale, so patient, night by night,
  Her eyes upon this pathway here,
Until at last I came in sight, —
  Nay, do not frown, my dear,

That was another world! and so
  Between us there can be no strife;
I was but twenty, you must know,
  And she my baby-wife!

Twin violets by a shady brook
  Were like her eyes, — their beauteousness
Was in a rainy, moonlight look
  Of tears and tenderness.

Her fingers had a dewy touch;
  Grace was in all her modest ways;
Forgive my praising her so much, —
  She cannot hear my praise.

Beneath the window where you see
  The trembling, tearful flowers, she lay,
Her arms as if they reached for me, —
  Her hair put smooth away.

The closéd mouth still smiling sweet,
  The waxen eyelids, drooping low,
The marriage-slippers on the feet, —
  The marriage-dress of snow!

And still, as in my dreams, I do,
  I kiss the sweet white hands, the eyes;
My heart with pain is broken anew,
  My soul with sorrow dies.

It was, they said, her spirit's birth, —
  That she was gone, a saint to be;
Alas! a poor, pale piece of earth
  Was all that I could see.

In tears, my darling! that fair brow
  With jealous shadows overrun?
A score of flowers upon one bough
  May bloom as well as one!

This ragged bush, from spring to fall,
  Stands here with living glories lit;
And every flower a-blush, with all
  That doth belong to it!

Look on it! learn the lesson then, —
  No more than we evoke, is ours!
The great law holdeth good with men,
  The same as with the flowers.

And if that lost, that sweet white hand
  Had never blessed me with its light,
You had not been, you understand,
  More than you are to-night.

This foolish pride that women have
  To play upon us, — to enthrall,
To absorb, doth hinder what they crave, —
  Their being loved at all!

Never the mistress of the arts
  They practise on us, still again
And o'er again, they wring our hearts
  With pain that giveth pain!

They make their tyranny a boast,
  And in their petulance will not see
That he is always bound the most,
  Who in the most is free!

They prize us more for what they screen
  From censure, than for what is best;
And you, my darling, at fifteen,
  Why, you are like the rest!

Your arms would find me now, though I
  Were low as ever guilt can fall;
And that, my little love, is why
  I love you, after all!

Smiling! "the pain is worth the cost,
  That wins a homily so wise?"
Ah, little tyrant, I am lost,
  When thus you tyrannize.

JENNY DUNLEATH.

JENNY DUNLEATH coming back to the town?
What! coming back here for good, and for all?
Well, that 's the last thing for Jenny to do, —
I 'd go to the ends of the earth, — would n't you?
Before I 'd come back! She 'll be pushed to the wall
Some slips, I can tell her, are never lived down,
And she ought to know it. It 's really true,
You think, that she 's coming? How dreadfully bold!
But one don't know what will be done, nowadays,
And Jenny was never the girl to be moved
By what the world said of her. What she approved,
She would do, in despite of its blame or its praise.

She ought to be wiser by this time — let 's see;
Why, sure as you live, she is forty years old!
The day I was married she stood up with me,
And *my* Kate is twenty: ah yes, it must be
That Jenny is forty, at least — forty-three,
It may be, or four. She was older, I know,
A good deal, when she was my bridesmaid, than I,
And that 's twenty years, now, and longer, ago;
So if she intends to come back and deny

Her age, as 't is likely she will, I can show
The plain honest truth, by the age of my Kate,
And I will, too! To see an old maid tell a lie,
Just to seem to be young, is a thing that I hate.

You thought we were friends? No, my dear, not at all!
'T is true we were friendly, as friendliness goes,
But one gets one's friends as one chooses one's clothes,
And just as the fashion goes out, lets them fall.
I will not deny we were often together
About the time Jenny was in her high feather;
And she *was* a beauty! No rose of the May
Looked ever so lovely as she on the day
I was married. She, somehow, could grace
Whatever thing touched her. The knots of soft lace
On her little white shoes, — the gay cap that half hid
Her womanly forehead, — the bright hair that slid
Like sunshine adown her bare shoulders, — the gauze
That rippled about her sweet arms, just because
'T was Jenny that wore it, — the flower in her belt, —
No matter what color, 't was fittest, you felt.
If she sighed, if she smiled, if she played with her fan,
A sort of religious coquettishness ran
Through it all, — a bewitching and wildering way,
All tearfully tender and graciously gay.
If e'er you were foolish in word or in speech,
The approval she gave with her serious eyes
Would make your own foolishness seem to you wise;
So all from her magical presence, and each,

Went happy away: 't was her art to confer
A self-love, that ended in your loving her.

And so she is coming back here! a mishap
To her friends, if she have any friends, one would say
Well, well, she can't take her old place in the lap
Of holiday fortune: her head must be gray;
And those dazzling cheeks! I would just like to see
How she looks, if I could, without her seeing me.

To think of the Jenny Dunleath that I knew,
A dreary old maid, with nobody to love her,—
Her hair silver-white and no roof-tree above her,—
One ought to have pity upon her,—'t is true!
But I never liked her; in truth, I was glad
In my own secret heart when she came to her fall;
When praise of her meekness was ringing the loudest
I always would say she was proud as the proudest;
That meekness was only a trick that she had,—
She was too proud to seem to be proud, that was all.

She stood up with me, I was saying: that day
Was the last of her going abroad for long years;
I never had seen her so bright and so gay,
Yet, spite of the lightness, I had my own fears
That all was not well with her: 't was but her pride
Made her sing the old songs when they asked her to
sing,
For when it was done with, and we were aside,

A look wan and weary came over her brow,
And still I can feel just as if it were now,
How she slipped up and down on my finger, the ring,
And so hid her face in my bosom and cried.

When the fiddlers were come, and young Archibald Mill
Was dancing with Hetty, I saw how it was;
Nor was I misled when she said she was ill,
For the dews were not standing so thick in the grass
As the drops on her cheeks. So you never have heard
How she fell in disgrace with young Archibald! No?
I won't be the first, then, to whisper a word,—
Poor thing! if she only repent, let it go!

Let it go! let what go? My good madam, I pray,
Whereof do I stand here accused? I would know,—
I am Jenny Dunleath, that you knew long ago,
A dreary old maid, and unloved, as you say:
God keep you, my sister, from knowing such woe!
Forty years old, madam, that I agree,
The roses washed out of my cheeks by the tears;
And counting my barren and desolate years
By the bright little heads dropping over your knee,
You look on my sorrow with scorn, it appears.

Well, smile, if you can, as you hold up in sight
Your matronly honors, for all men to see;
But I cannot discern, madam, what there can be
To move your proud mirth, in the wildness of night

Falling round me ; no hearth for my coming alight, —
No rosy-red cheeks at the windows for me.

My love is my shame, — in your love you are crowned, —
But as we are women, our natures are one ;
By need of its nature, the dew and the sun
Belong to the poorest, pale flower o' the ground.
And think you that He who created the heart
Has struck it all helpless and hopeless apart
From these lesser works ? Nay, I hold He has bound
Our rights with our needs in so sacred a knot,
We cannot undo them with any mere lie ;
Nay, more, my proud lady, — the love you have got,
May belong to another as dreary as I !
You have all the world's recognition, — your bond, —
But have you that better right, lying beyond ? —
Agreement with Conscience ? — that sanction whereby
You can live in the face of the cruelest scorns ?
Ay, set your bare bosom against the sharp thorns
Of jealousy, hatred, — against all the harms
Bad fortune can gather, — and say, With these arms
About me, I stand here to live and to die !
I take you to keep for my patron and saint,
And you shall be bound by that sweetest constraint
Of a liberty wide as the love that you give ;
And so to the glory of God we will live,
Through health and through sickness, dear lover and
friend,
Through light and through darkness, — through all, to
the end !

Let it go! Let what go? Make me answer, I pray.
You were speaking just now of some terrible fall, —
My love for young Archibald Mill, — is that all?
I loved him with all my young heart, as you say, —
Nay, what is more, madam, I love him to-day, —
My cheeks thin and wan, and my hair gray on gray!
And so I am bold to come back to the town,
In hope that at last I may lay my bones down,
And have the green grasses blow over my face,
Among the old hills where my love had its birth!
If love were a trifle, the morning to grace,
And fade when the night came, why, what were it
worth?

He is married! and I am come hither too late?
Your vision misleads you, — so pray you, untie
That knot from your sweet brow, — I come here to die,
And not to make moan for the chances of fate!
I know that all love that is true is divine,
And when this low incident, Time, shall have sped,
I know the desire of my soul shall be mine, —
That, weary, or wounded, or dying, or dead,
The end is secure, so I bear the estate —
Despised of the world's favored women — and wait.

TRICKSEY'S RING.

O WHAT a day it was to us, —
  My wits were upside down,
When cousin Joseph Nicholas
  Came visiting from town!

His curls they were so smooth and bright,
  His frills they were so fine,
I thought perhaps the stars that night
  Would be ashamed to shine.

But when the dews had touched the grass,
  They came out, large and small,
As if our cousin Nicholas
  Had not been there at all!

Our old house never seemed to me
  So poor and mean a thing
As then, and just because that he
  Was come a-visiting!

I never thought the sun prolonged
  His light a single whit
Too much, till then, nor thought he wronged
  My face, by kissing it.

But now I sought to pull my dress
Of faded homespun down,
Because my cousin Nicholas
Would see my feet were brown.

The butterflies — bright airy things —
From off the lilac buds
I scared, for having on their wings
The shadows of the woods.

I thought my straight and jet black hair
Was almost a disgrace,
Since Joseph Nicholas had fair
Smooth curls about his face.

I wished our rosy window sprays
Were laces, dropping down,
That he might think we knew the ways
Of rich folks in the town.

I wished the twittering swallow had
A finer tune to sing,
Since such a stylish city lad
Was come a-visiting.

I wished the hedges, as they swayed,
Were each a solid wall,
And that our grassy lane were made
A market street withal.

I wished the drooping heads of rye,
  Set full of silver dews,
Were silken tassels all to tie
  The ribbons of his shoes!

And when, by homely household slight,
  They called me Tricksey True,
I thought my cheeks would blaze, in spite
  Of all that I could do.

Tricksey! — that name would surely be
  A shock to ears polite;
In short I thought that nothing we
  Could say or do was right.

For injured pride I could have wept,
  Until my heart and I
Fell musing how my mother kept
  So equable and high.

She did not cast her eyelids down,
  Ashamed of being poor;
To her a gay young man from town,
  Was no discomfiture.

She reverenced honor's sacred laws
  As much, ay more than he,
And was not put about because
  He had more gold than she;

But held her house beneath a hand
  As steady and serene,
As though it were a palace, and
  As though she were a queen.

And when she set our silver cup
  Upon the cloth of snow,
For Nicholas, I lifted up
  My timid eyes, I know;

And saw a ring, as needs I must,
  Upon his finger shine;
O how I longed to have it just
  A minute upon mine!

I thought of fairy folk that led
  Their lives in sylvan shades,
And brought fine things, as I had read,
  To little rustic maids.

And so I mused within my heart,
  How I would search about
The fields and woodlands, for my part,
  Till I should spy them out.

And so when down the western sky
  The sun had dropped at last,
Right softly and right cunningly
  From out the house I passed.

It was as if awake I dreamed,
  All Nature was so sweet
The small round dandelions seemed
  Like stars beneath my feet.

Fresh greenness as I went along
  The grass did seem to take,
And birds beyond the time of song
  Kept singing for my sake.

The dew o'erran the lily's cup,
  The ground-moss shone so well,
That if the sky were down or up,
  Was hard for me to tell.

I never felt my heart to sit
  So lightly on its throne;
Ah, who knew what would come of it,
  With fairy folk alone!

An hour, — another hour went by,
  All harmless arts I tried,
And tried in vain, and wearily
  My hopes within me died.

No tent of moonshine, and no ring
  Of dancers could I find, —
The fairy rich folk and their king
  For once would be unkind!

My spirit, nameless fear oppressed;
  My courage went adrift,
As all out of the low dark west
  The clouds began to lift.

I lost my way within the wood, —
  The path I could not guess,
When, Heaven be praised, before me stood
  My cousin Nicholas!

Right tenderly within his arm
  My shrinking hand he drew;
He spoke so low, "these damps will harm
  My little Tricksey True."

I know not how it was: my shame
  In new delight was drowned;
His accent gave my rustic name
  Almost a royal sound.

He bent his cheek against my face, —
  He whispered in my ear,
"Why came you to this dismal place?
  Tell me, my little dear!"

Betwixt the boughs that o'er us hung
  The light began to fall;
His praises loosed my silent tongue, —
  At last I told him all.

I felt his lips my forehead touch ;
  I shook and could not stand ;
The ring I coveted so much
  Was shining on my hand !

We talked about the little elves
  And fairies of the grove,
And then we talked about ourselves,
  And then we talked of love.

'T was at the ending of the lane, —
  The garden yet to pass,
I offered back his ring again
  To my good Nicholas.

" Dear Tricksey, don't you understand,
  You foolish little thing,"
He said, " that I must have the hand,
  As well as have the ring ? "

" To-night — just now ! I pray you wait !
  The hand is little worth ! "
" Nay darling — now ! we 're at the gate ! "
  And so he had them both !

CRAZY CHRISTOPHER.

NEIGHBORED by a maple wood,
  Dim and dusty, old and low;
Thus our little schoolhouse stood,-
  Two and twenty years ago.

On the roof of clapboards, dried
  Smoothly in the summer heat,
Of the hundred boys that tried,
  Never one could keep his feet.

Near the door the cross-roads were,
  A stone's throw, perhaps, away,
And to read the sign-board there,
  Made a pastime every day.

He who turned the index down,
  So it pointed on the sign
To the nearest market-town,
  Was, we thought, a painter fine;

And the childish wonder rose,
  As we gazed with puzzled looks
On the letters, good as those
  Printed in our spelling-books.

Near it was a well, — how deep!
  With its bucket warped and dry,
Broken curb, and leaning sweep,
  And a plum-tree growing by,

Which, with low and tangly top,
  Made the grass so bright and cool,
Travellers would sometimes stop,
  For a half-hour's rest — in school,

Not an eye could keep the place
  Of the lesson then, — intent
Each to con the stranger's face,
  And to see the road he went.

Scattered are we far and wide, —
  Careless, curious children then;
Wanderers some, and some have died;
  Some, thank God, are honest men.

But, as playmates, large or small,
  Noisy, thoughtful, or demure,
I can see them, one and all,
  The great world in miniature.

Common flowers, with common names,
  Filled the woods and meadows round:
Dandelions with their flames
  Smothered flat against the ground;

Mullein stocks, with gray braids set
  Full of yellow; thistles, speared;
Violets, purple near to jet;
  Crowfoot, and the old-man's-beard.

And along the dusty way,
  Thick as prints of naked feet,
Iron-weeds and fennel gay
  Blossomed in the summer heat.

Hedges of wild blackberries,
  Pears, and honey-locusts tall,
Spice-wood, and "good apple-trees,"
  Well enough we knew them all.

But the ripest blackberries,
  Nor the mulleins topped with gold,
Peach nor honey-locust trees,
  Nor the flowers, when all are told,

Pleased us like the cabin, near
  Which a silver river ran,
And where lived, for many a year,
  Christopher, the crazy man.

Hair as white as snow he had,
  Mixing with a beard that fell
Down his breast; if he were mad,
  Passed our little wits to tell.

In his eyes' unfathomed blue
  Burned a ray so clear and bright,
Oftentimes we said we knew
  It would shame the candlelight.

Mystic was the life he led;
  Picking herbs in secret nooks, —
Finding, as the old folks said,
  "Tongues in trees and books in brooks."

Waking sometimes in the gloom
  Of the solemn middle night,
He had seen his narrow room
  Full of angels dressed in white;

So he said in all good faith,
  And one day, with tearful eye,
Told us that he heard old Death
  Sharpening his scythe, close by.

Whether it were prophecy,
  Or a dream, I cannot say;
But good little Emily
  Died the evening of that day.

In the woods, where up and down
  We had searched, and only seen
Adder's-tongue, with dull, dead brown,
  Mottled with the heavy green;

May-apples, or wild birds sweet,
  Going through the shadows dim,
Spirits, with white, noiseless feet,
  Walked, he said, and talked with him.

"What is all the toiling for,
  And the spinning?" he would say;
"See the lilies at my door, —
  Never dressed a queen as they.

"He who gives the ravens food
  For our wants as well will care;
O my children! He is good, —
  Better than your fathers are."

So he lived from year to year,
  Never toiling, mystery-clad, —
Spirits, if they did appear,
  Being all the friends he had.

Alternating seasons sped,
  And there fell no night so rough,
But his cabin fire, he said,
  Made it light and warm enough.

Soft and slow our steps would be,
  As the silver river ran,
Days when we had been to see
  Christopher, the crazy man.

Soft and slow, to number o'er
  The delights he said he had;
Wondering always, more and more,
  Whether he were wise or mad.

On a hill-side next the sun,
  Where the schoolboys quiet keep,
And to seed the clovers run,
  He is lying, fast asleep.

But at last, (to Heaven be praise,)
  Gabriel his bed will find,
Giving love for lonely days,
  And for visions, his right mind.

Sometimes, when I think about
  How he lived among the flowers,
Gently going in and out,
  With no cares nor fretful hours, —

Of the deep serene of light,
  In his blue, unfathomed eyes, —
Seems the childish fancy right,
  That could half believe him wise.

THE FERRY OF GALLAWAY.

In the stormy waters of Gallaway
My boat had been idle the livelong day,
Tossing and tumbling to and fro,
For the wind was high and the tide was low.

The tide was low and the wind was high,
And we were heavy, my heart and I,
For not a traveller all the day
Had crossed the ferry of Gallaway.

At set o' th' sun, the clouds outspread
Like wings of darkness overhead,
When, out o' th' west, my eyes took heed
Of a lady, riding at full speed.

The hoof-strokes struck on the flinty hill
Like silver ringing on silver, till
I saw the veil in her fair hand float,
And flutter a signal for my boat.

The waves ran backward as if 'ware
Of a presence more than mortal fair,
And my little craft leaned down and lay
With her side to th' sands o' th' Gallaway.

"Haste, good boatman! haste!" she cried,
"And row me over the other side!"
And she stript from her finger the shining ring,
And gave it me for the ferrying.

"Woe 's me! my Lady, I may not go,
For the wind is high and th' tide is low,
And rocks like dragons lie in the wave, —
Slip back on your finger the ring you gave!"

"Nay, nay! for the rocks will be melted down,
And the waters, they never will let me drown,
And the wind a pilot will prove to thee,
For my dying lover, he waits for me!"

Then bridle-ribbon and silver spur
She put in my hand, but I answered her:
"The wind is high and the tide is low, —
I must not, dare not, and will not go!"

Her face grew deadly white with pain,
And she took her champing steed by th' mane,
And bent his neck to th' ribbon and spur
That lay in my hand, — but I answered her:

"Though you should proffer me twice and thrice
Of ring and ribbon and steed, the price, —
The leave of kissing your lily-like hand!
I never could row you safe to th' land."

"Then God have mercy!" she faintly cried,
"For my lover is dying the other side!
O cruel, O cruellest Gallaway,
Be parted, and make me a path, I pray!"

Of a sudden, the sun shone large and bright
As if he were staying away the night,
And the rain on the river fell as sweet
As the pitying tread of an angel's feet.

And spanning the water from edge to edge
A rainbow stretched like a golden bridge,
And I put the rein in her hand so fair,
And she sat in her saddle, th' queen o' th' air.

And over the river, from edge to edge,
She rode on the shifting and shimmering bridge,
And landing safe on the farther side, —
"Love is thy conqueror, Death!" she cried.

Our unwise purposes are wisely crossed;
Being small ourselves, we must essay small things:
Th' adventurous mote, with wide, outwearied wings
Crawling across a water-drop, is lost.

REVOLUTIONARY STORY.

"Good mother, what quaint legend are you reading,
In that old-fashioned book?
Beside your door I 've been this half-hour pleading
All vainly for one look.

"About your chair the little birds fly bolder
Than in the woods they fly,
With heads dropt slantwise, as if o'er your shoulder
They read as they went by;

"Each with his glossy collar ruffling double
Around his neck so slim,
Even as with that atmosphere of trouble,
Through which our blessings swim.

"Is it that years throw on us chillier shadows,
The longer time they run,
That, with your sad face fronting yonder meadows,
You creep into the sun?

"I 'll sit upon the ground and hear your story."
Sadly she shook her head,
And, pushing back the thin, white veil of glory
'Twixt her and heaven, she said:

"Ah! wondering child, I knew not of your pleading;
  My thoughts were chained, indeed,
Upon my book, and yet what you call reading
  I have no skill to read.

"There was a time once when I had a lover;
  Why look you in such doubt?
True, I am old now — ninety years and over:"
  A crumpled flower fell out

From 'twixt the book-leaves. "Seventy years they 've pressed it:
  'T was like a living flame,
When he that plucked it, by the plucking blessed it:"
  I knew the smile that came,

And flickered on her lips in wannish splendor,
  Was lighted at that flower,
For even yet its radiance, faint and tender,
  Reached to its primal hour.

"God bless you! seventy years since it was gathered?'
  "Ay, I remember well;"
And in her old hand, palsy-struck, and withered,
  She held it up to smell.

"And is it true, as poets say, good mother,
  That love can never die?
And that for all it gives unto another
  It grows the richer?" "Ay,

"The wild wall-brier, from spring till summer closes,
  All the great world around,
Hangs by its thorny arms to keep its roses
  From off the low, black ground;

"And love is like it: sufferings but try it;
  Death but evokes the might
That, all too mighty to be thwarted by it,
  Breaks through into the light."

"Then frosty age may wrap about its bosom
  The light of fires long dead?"
Kissing the piece of dust she called a blossom,
  She shut the book, and said:

"You see yon ash-tree with its thick leaves, blowing
  The blue side out? (Great Power,
Keep its head green!) My sweetheart, in the mowing,
  Beneath it found my flower.

"A mile off all that day the shots were flying,
  And mothers, from the door,
Looked for the sons, who, on their faces lying,
  Would come home never more.

"Across the battle-field the dogs went whining;
  I saw, from where I stood,
Horses with quivering flanks, and strained eyes, shining
  Like thin skins full of blood.

"Brave fellows we had then: there was my neighbor, —
  The British lines he saw;
Took his old scythe and ground it to a sabre,
  And mowed them down like straw!

"And there were women, then, of giant spirit, —
  Nay, though the blushes start,
The garments their degenerate race inherit
  Hang loose about the heart.

"Where was I, child? how is my story going?"
  "Why, where by yonder tree
With leaves so rough your sweetheart, in the mowing,
  Gathered your flower!" "Ah me!

"My poor lad dreamed not of the red-coat devil,
  That, just for pastime, drew
To his bright epaulet his musket level,
  And shot him through and through.

"Beside him I was kneeling the next minute;
  From the red grass he took
The shattered hand up, and the flower was in it
  You saw within my book."

"He died." "Then you have seen some stormy weather?"
  "Ay, more of foul than fair;
And all the snows we should have shared together
  Have fallen on my hair."

"And has your life been worth the living, mother,
 With all its sorrows?" "Ay,
I 'd live it o'er again, were there no other,
 For this one memory."

I answered soft, — I felt the place was holy, —
 One maxim stands approved:
"They know the best of life, however lowly,
 Who ever have been loved."

Just here and there with some poor little ray
 Of lovely sort, the web of life is crossed;
Where a good impulse found in action play, —
 Where a true word was said: the rest is lost.

HOPE in our hearts doth only stay
  Like a traveller at an inn,
Who riseth up at the break of day
  His journey to begin.

Faith, when her soul has known the blight
  Of noisy doubts and fears,
Goes thenceforward clad in the light
  Of the still eternal years.

Truth is Truth: no *more* in the prayers
  Of the righteous Pharisee;
No *less* in the humblest sinner that wears
  This poor mortality.

But Love is greatest of all: no loss
  Can shadow its face with gloom, —
As glorious hanging on the cross
  As breaking out of the tomb.

Thoughts and Theories.

THANKSGIVING.

For the sharp conflicts I have had with sin,
Wherein
I have been wedged and pressed
Nigh unto death, I thank Thee, with the rest
Of my befallings, Lord, of brighter guise,
And named by mortals, good,
Which to my hungry heart have given food,
Or costly entertainment to my eyes.

For I can only see,
With spirit truly reconciled to Thee,
In the sad evils with our lives that blend,
A means, and not an end:

Since Thou wert free
To do thy will — knewest the bitter worth
Of sin, and all its possibility,
Ere that, by thy decree,

The ancient silence of eternity
Was broken by the music of man's birth.

Therefore I lay my brows
Discrowned of youth, within thy gracious hands,
Or rise while daybreak dew is on the boughs
To strew thy road with sweets, for thy commands
Do make the current of my life to run
Through lost and cavernous ways,
Bordered with cloudy days,
In its slow working out into the sun.

Hills, clap your hands, and all ye mountains, shout;
Hie, fainting hart, to where the waters flow;
Children of men, put off your fear and doubt;
The Lord who chasteneth, loveth you, for, lo!
The wild herb's wounded stalk He cares about,
And shields the ravens when the rough winds blow;
He sendeth down the drop of shining dew
To light the daisy from her house of death,
And shall He, then, forget the like of you,
O ye, of little faith!

He speaketh to the willing soul and heart
By dreams, and in the visions of the night,
And happy is the man who, for his part,
Rejoiceth in the light
Of all His revelations, whether found
In the old books, so sacredly upbound,

And clasped with golden clasps, or whether writ
Through later instillations of His power,
Where he that runneth still perceiveth it
Illuminating every humble flower
That springeth from the ground.

His testimony all the time is sure;
The smallest star that keepeth in the night
His silver candle bright,
And every deed of good that anywhere
Maketh the hands of holy women white;
All sweet religious work, all earnest prayer,
Of uttered, or unutterable speech;
Whatever things are peaceable and pure,
Whatever things are right,
These are His witnesses, ay, all and each!

Thrice happy is the man who doth obey
The Lord of Love, through love; who fears to break
The righteous law for th' law's righteous sake;
And who, by daily use of blessings, gives
Thanks for the daily blessings he receives;
His spirit grown so reverent, it dares
Cast the poor shows of reverence away,
Believing they
More glorify the Giver, who partake
Of His good gifts, than they who fast and make
Burnt offerings and Pharisaic prayers.

The wintry snows that blind
The air, and blight what things were glorified
By summer's reign, we do not think unkind
When that we see them changed, afar and wide,
To rain, that, fretting in the rose's face,
Brings out a softer grace,
And makes the troops of rustic daffodils
Shake out their yellow skirts along the hills,
And all the valleys blush from side to side.

And as we climb the stair
Of rough and ugly fortune, by the props
Of faith and charity, and hope and prayer,
To the serene and beauteous mountain-tops
Of our best human possibility,
Where haunts the spirit of eternity,
The world below looks fair, —
Its seeming inequalities subdued,
And level, all, to purposes of good.

I thank thee, Gracious Lord,
For the divine award
Of strength that helps me up the heavy heights
Of mortal sorrow, where, through tears forlorn,
My eyes get glimpses of the authentic lights
Of love's eternal morn.

For thereby do I trust
That our afflictions spring not from the dust,

And that they are not sent
In arbitrary chastisement,
Nor as avengers to put out the light
And let our souls loose in some damnéd night
That holds the balance of thy glory, just;
But rather, that as lessons they are meant,
And as the fire tempers the iron, so
Are we refined by woe.

I thank Thee for my common blessings, still
Rained through thy will
Upon my head; the air
That knows so many tunes which grief beguile,
Breathing its light love to me everywhere,
And that will still be kissing all the while.

I thank Thee that my childhood's vanished days
Were cast in rural ways,
Where I beheld, with gladness ever new,
That sort of vagrant dew
Which lodges in the beggarly tents of such
Vile weeds as virtuous plants disdain to touch,
And with rough-bearded burs, night after night,
Upgathered by the morning, tender and true,
Into her clear, chaste light.

Such ways I learned to know
That free will cannot go
Outside of mercy; learned to bless His name

Whose revelations, ever thus renewed
Along the varied year, in field and wood,
His loving care proclaim.

I thank Thee that the grass and the red rose
Do what they can to tell
How spirit through all forms of matter flows;
For every thistle by the common way
Wearing its homely beauty, — for each spring
That sweet and homeless, runneth where it will, —
For night and day,
For the alternate seasons, — everything
Pertaining to life's marvellous miracle.

Even for the lowly flower
That, living, dwarfed and bent
Under some beetling rock, in gloom profound,
Far from her pretty sisters of the ground,
And shut from sun and shower,
Seemeth endowed with human discontent.

Ah! what a tender hold
She taketh of us in our own despite, —
A sadly-solemn creature,
Crooked, despoiled of nature,
Leaning from out the shadows, dull and cold,
To lay her little white face in the light.

The chopper going by her rude abode,

Thinks of his own rough hut, his old wife's smile,
And of the bare young feet
That run through th' frost to meet
His coming, and forgets the weary load
Of sticks that bends his shoulders down the while.

I thank thee, Lord, that Nature is so wise,
So capable of painting in men's eyes
Pictures whose airy hues
Do blend and interfuse
With all the darkness that about us lies, —
That clearly in our hearts
Her law she writes,
Reserving cunning past our mortal arts,
Whereby she is avenged for all her slights.

And I would make thanksgiving
For the sweet, double living,
That gives the pleasures that have passed away,
The sweetness and the sunshine of to-day.

I see the furrows ploughed and see them planted,
See the young cornstalks rising green and fair;
Mute things are friendly, and I am acquainted
With all the luminous creatures of the air;
And with the cunning workers of the ground
That have their trades born with them, and with all
The insects, large and small,
That fill the Summer with a wave of sound.

I watch the wood-bird line
Her pretty nest, with eyes that never tire,
And watch the sunbeams trail their wisps of fire
Along the bloomless bushes, till they shine.

The violet, gathering up her tender blue
From th' dull ground, is a good sight to see ;
And it delighteth me
To have the mushroom push his round head through
The dry and brittle stubble, as I pass,
His smooth and shining coat, half rose half fawn,
But just put on ;
And to have April slip her showery grass
Under my feet, as she was used to do,
In the dear Spring-times gone.

I make the brook, my Nile,
And hour by hour beguile,
Tracking its devious course
Through briery banks to its mysterious source,
That I discover, always, at my will, —
A little silver star,
Under the shaggy forehead of some hill,
From travelled ways afar.

Forgetting wind and flood,
I build my house of unsubstantial sand,
Shaping the roof upon my double hand,
And setting up the dry and sliding grains,

With infinite pains,
In the similitude
Of beam and rafter, — then
Where to the ground the dock its broad leaf crooks,
I hunt long whiles to find the little men
That I have read of in my story-books.

Often, in lawless wise,
Some obvious work of duty I delay,
Taking my fill
Of an uneasy liberty, and still
Close shutting up my eyes,
As though it were not given me to see
The avenging ghost of opportunity
Thus slighted, far away.

I linger when I know
That I should forward go;
Now, haply for the katydid's wild shrill,
Now listening to the low,
Dull noise of mill-wheels — counting, now, the row
Of clouds about the shoulder of the hill.

My heart anew rejoices
In th' old familiar voices
That come back to me like a lullaby;
Now 't is the church-bell's call,
And now a teamster's whistle, — now, perhaps,
The silvery lapse

Of waters in among the reeds that meet;
  And now, down-dropping to a whispery fall,
Some milkmaid, chiding with love's privilege,
    Through the green wall
    Of the dividing hedge,
And the so sadly eloquent reply
Of the belated cow-boy, low and sweet.

    I see, as in a dream,
    The farmer plodding home behind his team,
With all the tired shadows following,
And see him standing in his threshing-floor,
The hungry cattle gathered in a ring
    About the great barn-door.

    I see him in the sowing,
    And see him in the mowing,
The air about him thick with gray-winged moths;
    The day's work nearly over,
And the long meadow ridged with double swaths
    Of sunset-light and clover.

When falls the time of solemn Sabbath rest,
    In all he has of best
I see him going (for he never fails)
To church, in either equitable hand
A shining little one, and all his band
Trooping about him like a flock of quails.

With necks bowed low, and hid to half their length
Under the jutting load of new-made hay,
I see the oxen give their liberal strength
Day after day,
And see the mower stay
His scythe, and leave a patch of grass to spread
Its shelter round the bed
Of the poor frighted ground-bird in his way.

I see the joyous vine,
And see the wheat set up its rustling spears,
And see the Sun with golden fingers sign
The promise of full ears.

I see the slender Moon
Time after time grow old and round in th' face,
And see the Autumn take the Summer's place,
And shake the ripe nuts down,
In their thick, bitter hulls of green and brown,
To make the periods of the school-boy's tune ;
I see the apples, with their russet cheeks
Shaming the wealth of June ;
And see the bean-pods, gay with purple freaks,
And all the hills with yellow leaves o'erblown,
As through the fading woods I walk alone,
And hear the wind o'erhead
Touching the joyless boughs and making moan,
Like some old crone,
Who on her withered fingers counts her dead.

I hear the beetle's hum, and see the gnats
Sagging along the air in strings of jet,
And from their stubs I see the weak-eyed bats
Flying an hour before the Sun is set.
        Picture on picture crowds,
And by the gray and priestlike silence led,
Comes the first star through evening's steely gates
        And chides the day to bed
Within the ruddy curtains of the clouds;
        So gently com'st thou, Death,
        To him who waits,
In the assurance of our blessed faith,
To be acquainted with thy quiet arms,
        His good deeds, great and small,
        Builded about him like a silver wall,
And bearing back the deluge of alarms.

The mother doth not tenderer appear
When, from her heart her tired darling laid,
She trims his cradle all about with shade,
And will not kiss his sleepy eyes for fear.

I see the windows of the homestead bright
        With the warm evening-light,
        And by the winter-fire
        I see the gray-haired sire
        Serenely sitting,
Forgetful of the work-day toil and care,
The old wife by his elbow, at her knitting;

The cricket on the hearth-stone singing shrill,
And the spoiled darling of the house at will
Climbing the good man's chair,
A furtive glimpse to catch
Of her fair face in his round silver watch,
That she in her high privilege must wear,
And listen to the music that is in it,
Though only for a minute.

I thank thee, Lord, for every saddest cross;
Gain comes to us through loss,
The while we go,
Blind travellers holding by the wall of time,
And seeking out through woe
The things that are eternal and sublime.

Ah! sad are they of whom no poet writes
Nor ever any story-teller hears, —
The childless mothers, who on lonesome nights
Sit by their fires and weep, having the chores
Done for the day, and time enough to see
All the wide floors
Swept clean of playthings; they, as needs must be,
Have time enough for tears.

But there are griefs more sad
Than ever any childless mother had, —
You know them, who do smother Nature's cries
Under poor masks

Of smiling, slow despair, —
Who put your white and unadorning hair
Out of your way, and keep at homely tasks,
Unblest with any praises of men's eyes,
Till Death comes to you with his piteous care,
And to unmarriageable beds you go,
Saying, "It is not much; 't is well, if so
We only be made fair
And looks of love await us when we rise."

My cross is not as hard as theirs to bear,
And yet alike to me are storms, or calms;
My life's young joy,
The brown-cheeked farmer-boy,
Who led the daisies with him like his lambs, —
Carved his sweet picture on my milking-pail,
And cut my name upon his thrashing-flail,
One day stopped singing at his plough; alas!
Before that summer-time was gone, the grass
Had choked the path which to the sheep-field led,
Where I had watched him tread
So oft on evening's trail, —
A shining oat-sheaf balanced on his head,
And nodding to the gale.

Rough wintry weather came, and when it sped,
The emerald wave
Swelling above my little sweetheart's grave,
With such bright, bubbly flowers was set about,

I thought he blew them out,
And so took comfort that he was not dead.

For I was of a rude and ignorant crew,
And hence believed whatever things I saw
Were the expression of a hidden law;
And, with a wisdom wiser than I knew,
Evoked the simple meanings out of things
By childlike questionings.

And he they named with shudderings of fear
Had never, in his life, been half so near
As when I sat all day with cheeks unkissed,
And listened to the whisper, very low,
That said our love above death's wave of woe
Was joined together like the seamless mist.

God's yea and nay
Are not so far away,
I said, but I can hear them when I please:
Nor could I understand
Their doubting faith, who only touch His hand
Across the blind, bewildering centuries.

And often yet, upon the shining track
Of the old faith, come back
My childish fancies, never quite subdued;
And when the sunset shuts up in the wood
The whispery sweetness of uncertainty,

And Night, with misty locks that loosely drop
About his ears, brings rest, a welcome boon,
Playing his pipe with many a starry stop
That makes a golden snarling in his tune;

I see my little lad
Under the leafy shelter of the boughs,
Driving his noiseless, visionary cows,
Clad in a beauty I alone can see:
Laugh, you, who never had
Your dead come back, but do not take from me
The harmless comfort of my foolish dream,
That these, our mortal eyes,
Which outwardly reflect the earth and skies
Do introvert upon eternity:

And that the shapes you deem
Imaginations, just as clearly fall;
Each from its own divine original,
And through some subtle element of light,
Upon the inward, spiritual eye,
As do the things which round about them lie,
Gross and material, on the external sight.

THE BRIDAL VEIL.

We 're married, they say, and you think you have
won me, —
Well, take this white veil from my head, and look on me:
Here 's matter to vex you, and matter to grieve you,
Here 's doubt to distrust you, and faith to believe you, —
I am all as you see, common earth, common dew;
Be wary, and mould me to roses, not rue!

Ah! shake out the filmy thing, fold after fold,
And see if you have me to keep and to hold, —
Look close on my heart — see the worst of its sinning —
It is not yours to-day for the yesterday's winning —
The past is not mine — I am too proud to borrow —
You must grow to new heights if I love you to-morrow.

We 're married! I 'm plighted to hold up your praises,
As the turf at your feet does its handful of daisies;
That way lies my honor, — my pathway of pride,
But, mark you, if greener grass grow either side,
I shall know it, and keeping in body with you,
Shall walk in my spirit with feet on the dew!

We 're married! Oh, pray that our love do not fail!
I have wings flattened down and hid under my veil:
They are subtle as light — you can never undo them,
And swift in their flight — you can never pursue them,
And spite of all clasping, and spite of all bands,
I can slip like a shadow, a dream, from your hands.

Nay, call me not cruel, and fear not to take me,
I am yours for my lifetime, to be what you make me, —
To wear my white veil for a sign, or a cover,
As you shall be proven my lord, or my lover;
A cover for peace that is dead, or a token
Of bliss that can never be written or spoken.

THE SPECIAL DARLING

ALONG the grassy lane one day,
Outside the dull old-fashioned town,
A dozen children were at play;
From noontide till the even-fall,
Curly-heads flaxen and curly-heads brown
Were busily bobbing up and down
Behind the blackberry-wall.

And near these merry-makers wild
A piteous little creature was,
With face unlike the face of a child,—
Eyes fixed, and seeming frozen still,
And legs all doubled up in th' grass,
Disjointed from his will.

No dream deceived his dreary hours,
Nor made him merry nor made him grave;
He did not hear the children call,
Tumbling under the blackberry-wall,
With shoulders white with flowers;
But sat with great wide eyes one way,
And body limberly asway,
Like a water-plant in a wave.

He did not hear the little stir
The ants made, working in their hills,

Nor see the pale, gray daffodils
Lifting about him their dull points,
Nor yet the curious grasshopper
Transport his green and angular joints
From bush to bush. Poor simple boy, —
His senses cheated of their birth,
He might as well have grown in th' earth,
For all he knew of joy.

Near where the children took their fill
Of play, outside the dull old town,
And neighbored by a wide-flanked hill,
Where mists like phantoms up and down
Moved all the time, a homestead was,
With window toward the plot of grass
Where sat this child, and oft and again
Tender eyes peered through the pane,
Whose glances still were dim,
Till leaping over the blackberry-wall,
Curly-heads flaxen, brown and all,
They rested at last on him.

Ah, who shall say but that such love
Is the type of His who made us all,
And that from the Kingdom up above
The eyes that note the sparrow's fall,
O'er the incapable, weak and small,
Watch with tenderest care:
Such is my hope and prayer.

A DREAM OF THE WEST.

SUNSET! a hush is in the air, —
Their gray old heads the mountains bare,
As if the winds were saying prayer.

The woodland, with its broad, green wing,
Shuts up the insect-whispering,
And lo! the Sea gets up to sing.

The last red splendor fades and dies,
And shadows one by one arise,
To light the candles of the skies.

O wildflowers, wet with silver dew!
O woods, with starlight shining through!
My heart is in the West, with you.

How well I know each shrub and tree,
Each climbing vine and brier I see;
Like friends they seem to welcome me.

Musing, I go along the streams,
Sweetly believing in my dreams,
For Fancy like a prophet seems.

Beside me soft steps tread the sod,
As in the twilights gone they trod,
And I unlearn my doubts, thank God.

Unlearn my doubts, forget my fears,
And that bad carelessness that sears,
And makes me older than my years.

I hear a dear, familiar tone,
A loving hand clasps close my own,
And earth seems made for me alone.

If I my fortunes could have planned,
I would not have let go that hand,
But they must fall who learn to stand

And how to blend life's varied hues,
What ill to find, what good to lose,
My Father knoweth best to choose.

ON SEEING A DROWNING MOTH.

Poor little moth! thy summer sports were done,
Had I not happened by this pool to lie;
But thou hast pierced my conscience very sore
With thy vain flounderings, so come ashore
In the safe hollow of my helpful hand,—
Rest thee a little on the warm, dry sand,
Then crawling out into the friendly sun,
As best thou mayest, get thy wet wings dry.

Ay, it has touched my conscience, little moth,
To see thy bright wings made for other use,
Haply for just a moment's chance abuse,
Dragging thee, thus, to death; yet am I loth
To heed the lesson, for I fain would lie
Along the margin of this water low
And watch the sunshine run in tender gleams
Down the gray elders — watch those flowers of light —
If flowers they be, and not the golden dreams
Left in her grassy pillows by the night, —
The dandelions, that trim the shadows so,
And watch the wild flag, with her eyes of blue
Wide open for the sun to look into, —
Her green skirts laid along the wind, and she,
As if to mar fair fortune wantonly,
Wading along the water, half her height.
Fain would I lie, with arms across my breast,
As quiet as yon wood-duck on her nest,
That sits the livelong day with ruffled quills,
Waiting to see the little yellow bills
Breach the white walls about them, — would that I
Could find out some sweet charm wherewith to buy
A too uneasy conscience, — then would Rest
Gather and fold me to itself; and last,
Forgetting the hereafter and the past,
My soul would have the present for its guest,
And grow immortal.

So, my little fool,
Thou 'rt back upon the water! Lord! how vain

The strife to save or man or moth from pain
Merited justly, — having thy wild way
To travel all the air, thou comest here
To try with spongy feet the treacherous pool;
Well, thou at least hast made one truth more clear, —
Men make their fate, and do not fate obey.

GOOD AND EVIL.

The evil that men do lives after them,
The good is oft interred with their bones.
JULIUS CÆSAR.

ONCE when the messenger that stays
For all, beside me stood,
I mused on what great Shakspeare says
Of evil and of good.

And shall the evil I have done
Live after me? I said;
When lo! a splendor like the sun
Shone round about my bed.

And a sweet spirit of the skies
Near me, yet all apart,
In whispers like the low wind's sighs,
Spake to my listening heart;

Saying, your poet, reverenced thus,
For once hath been unwise;
The good we do lives after us,
The evil 't is that dies!

Evil is earthy, of the earth,—
  A thing of pain and crime,
That scarcely sends a shadow forth
  Beyond the bounds of time.

But good, in substance, dwells above
  This discontented sphere,
Extending only, through God's love,
  Uncertain shadows here.

STROLLER'S SONG.

THE clouds all round the sky are black,
As it never would shine again;
But I 'll sling my wallet over my back,
And trudge in spite of the rain!

And if there rise no star to guide
My feet when day is gone,
I 'll shift my wallet the other side,
And trudge right on and on.

For this of a truth I always note,
And shape my course thereby,
That Nature has never an overcoat
To keep her furrows dry.

And how should the hills be clothed with grain,
The vales with flowers be crowned,
But for the chain of the silver rain
That draws them out of the ground!

So I will trudge with heart elate,
  And feet with courage shod,
For that which men call chance and fate
  Is the handiwork of God.

There 's time for the night as well as the morn,
  For the dark as the shining sky;
The grain of the corn and the flower unborn
  Have rights as well as I.

A LESSON.

ONE Autumn-time I went into the woods
When Nature grieves,
And wails the drying up of the bright floods
Of Summer leaves.

The rose had drawn the green quilt of the grass
Over her head,
And, taking off her pretty, rustling dress,
Had gone to bed.

And, while the wind went ruffling through her bower
To do her harm,
She lay and slept away the frosty hour,
All safe and warm.

The little bird that came when May was new,
And sang her best,
Had gone, — I put my double hand into
Her chilly nest.

Then, sitting down beneath a naked tree,
I looked about, —
Saying, in these, if there a lesson be,
I 'll spy it out.

And presently the teaching that was meant
I thought I saw, —
That I, in trial, should patiently consent
To God's great law.

ON SEEING A WILD BIRD.

Beautiful symbol of a freer life,
  Knowing no purpose, and yet true to one;
  Would I could learn thy wisdom, I who run
This way and that, striving against my strife.

No fancy vague, no object half unknown,
  Diverts thee from thyself. By stops and starts
  I live the while by little broken parts
A thousand lives, — not one of all, my own.

Thou sing'st thy full heart out, and low or high
  Flyest at pleasure; who of us can say
  He lives his inmost self e'en for a day,
And does the thing he would? alas, not I.

We hesitate, go backward, and return,
  And when the earth with living sunshine gleams
  We make a darkness round us with our dreams,
And wait for that which we ourselves should earn.

For we shall work out answers to our needs
  If we have continuity of will
  To hold our shifting purposes until
They germinate, and bring forth fruit in deeds.

We ask and hope too much, — too lightly press
  Toward the end sought, and haply learn, at length,
  That we have vainly dissipated strength
Which, concentrated, would have brought success.

But Truth is sure, and can afford to wait
  Our slow perception, (error ebbs and flows;)
  Her essence is eternal, and she knows
The world must swing round to her, soon or late.

RICH, THOUGH POOR.

RED in the east the morning broke,
And in three chambers three men woke;
One through curtains wove that night
In the loom of the spider, saw the light
Lighting the rafters black and old,
And sighed for the genii to make them gold.

One in a chamber, high and fair,
With panelled ceilings, enamelled rare,
On the purple canopy of his bed
Saw the light with a sluggard's dread,
And buried his sullen and sickly face
Deep in his pillow fringed with lace.

One, from a low and grassy bed,
With the golden air for a coverlet;
No ornaments had he to wear
But his curling beard and his coal-black hair;
His wealth was his acres, and oxen twain,
And health was his cheerful chamberlain.

Night fell stormy — "Woe is me!"
Sighed so wearily two of the three;
"The corn I planted to-day will sprout,"
Said one, "and the roses be blushing out;"
And his heart with its joyful hope o'erran:
Think you he was the poorest man?

21

SIXTEEN.

Suppose your hand with power supplied, —
Say, would you slip it 'neath my hair,
And turn it to the golden side
Of sixteen years? Suppose you dare?

And I stood here with smiling mouth,
Red cheeks, and hands all softly white,
Exceeding beautiful with youth,
And that some sly, consenting sprite,

Brought dreams as bright as dreams can be,
To keep the shadows from my brow,
And plucked down hearts to pleasure me,
As you would roses from a bough;

What could I do then? idly wear —
While all my mates went on before —
The bashful looks and golden hair
Of sixteen years, and nothing more!

Nay, done with youth is my desire,
To Time I give no false abuse,
Experience is the marvellous fire
That welds our knowledge into use.

And all its fires of heart, or brain,
Where purpose into power was wrought,
I 'd bear, and gladly bear again,
Rather than be put back one thought.

So sigh no more, my gentle friend,
That I have reached the time of day
When white hairs come, and heart-beats send
No blushes through the cheeks astray.

For, could you mould my destiny
As clay within your loving hand,
I 'd leave my youth's sweet company,
And suffer back to where I stand.

PRAYER FOR LIGHT.

O WHAT is Thy will toward us mortals,
Most Holy and High?
Shall we die unto life while we 're living?
Or live while we die?

Can we serve Thee and wait on Thee only
In cells, dark and low?
Must the altars we build Thee be built with
The stones of our woe?

Shall we only attain the great measures
Of grace and of bliss
In the life that awaits us, by cruelly
Warring on this?

Or, may we still watch while we work, and
Be glad while we pray?
So reverent, we cast the poor shows of
Our reverence away!

Shall the nature Thou gav'st us, pronouncing it
Good, and not ill,
Be warped by our pride or our passion
Outside of Thy will?

Shall the sins which we do in our blindness
  Thy mercy transcend,
And drag us down deeper and deeper
  Through worlds without end?

Or, are we stayed back in sure limits,
  And Thou, high above,
O'erruling our trials for our triumph,
  Our hatreds for love?

And is each soul rising, though slowly,
  As onward it fares,
And are life's good things and its evil
  The steps in the stairs?

All day with my heart and my spirit,
  In fear and in awe,
I strive to feel out through my darkness
  Thy light and Thy law.

And this, when the sun from his shining
  Goes sadly away,
And the moon looketh out of her chamber,
  Is all I can say;

That He who foresaw of transgression
  The might and the length,
Has fashioned the law to exceed not
  Our poor human strength!

THE UNCUT LEAF.

You think I do not love you! Why,
  Because I have my secret grief?
Because in reading I pass by,
  Time and again, the uncut leaf?

One rainy night you read to me
  In some old book, I know not what,
About the woods of Eldersie,
  And a great hunt — I have forgot

What all the story was — ah, well,
  It touched me, and I felt the pain
With which the poor dumb creature fell
  To his weak knees, then rose again,

And shuddering, dying, turned about,
  Lifted his antlered head in pride,
And from his wounded face shook out
  The bloody arrows ere he died!

That night I almost dared, I think,
  To cut the leaf, and let the sun
Shine in upon the mouldy ink, —
  You ask me why it was not done.

Because I rather feel than know
  The truth which every soul receives
From kindred souls, that long ago
  You read me through the double leaves!

So pray you, leave my tears to blot
  The record of my secret grief,
And though I know you know, seem not
  Ever to see the uncut leaf.

THE MIGHT OF TRUTH.

We are proclaimed, even against our wills —
  If we are silent, then our silence speaks —
Children from tumbling on the summer-hills
  Come home with roses rooted in their cheeks.
I think no man can make his lie hold good, —
One way or other, truth is understood.

The still sweet influence of a life of prayer
  Quickens their hearts who never bow the knee, —
So come fresh draughts of living inland air
  To weary homesick men, far out at sea.
Acquaint thyself with God, O man, and lo!
His light shall, like a garment, round thee flow.

The selfishness that with our lives has grown,
  Though outward grace its full expression bar,
Will crop out here and there like belts of stone
  From shallow soil, discovering what we are.
The thing most specious cannot stead the true, —
Who would appear clean, must be clean all through

In vain doth Satan say, "My heart is glad,
  I wear of Paradise the morning gem;"
While on his brow, magnificently sad,
  Hangs like a crag his blasted diadem.
Still doth the truth the hollow lie invest,
And all the immortal ruin stands confessed.

COUNSEL.

Though sin hath marked thy brother's brow
  Love him in sin's despite,
But for his darkness, haply thou
  Hadst never known the light.

Be thou an angel to his life,
  And not a demon grim, —
Since with himself he is at strife,
  O be at peace with him.

Speak gently of his evil ways
  And all his pleas allow,
For since he knows not why he strays
  From virtue, how shouldst thou?

Love him, though all thy love he slights,
  For ah, thou canst not say
But that his prayerless days and nights
  Have taught thee how to pray.

Outside themselves all things have laws,
  The atom and the sun, —
Thou art thyself, perhaps, the cause
  Of sins which he has done.

If guiltless thou, why surely then
  Thy place is by his side, —
It was for sinners, not just men,
  That Christ the Saviour died.

THE LITTLE BLACKSMITH.

WE heard his hammer all day long
  On the anvil ring and ring,
But he always came when the sun went down
  To sit on the gate and sing.

His little hands so hard and brown
  Crossed idly on his knee,
And straw-hat lopping over cheeks
  As red as they could be;

His blue and faded jacket trimmed
  With signs of work, — his feet
All bare and fair upon the grass,
  He made a picture sweet.

For still his shoes, with iron shod,
  On the smithy-wall he hung;
As forth he came when the sun went down,
  And sat on the gate and sung.

The whistling rustic tending cows,
  Would keep in pastures near,
And half the busy villagers
  Lean from their doors to hear.

And from the time the bluebirds came
  And made the hedges bright,
Until the stubble yellow grew,
  He never missed a night.

The hammer's stroke on the anvil filled
  His heart with a happy ring,
And that was why, when the sun went down,
  He came to the gate to sing.

TWO TRAVELLERS.

Two travellers, meeting by the way,
Arose, and at the peep of day
Brake bread, paid reckoning, and they say

Set out together, and so trode
Till where upon the forking road
A gray and good old man abode.

There each began his heart to strip,
And all that light companionship
That cometh of the eye and lip

Had sudden end, for each began
To ask the gray and good old man
Whither the roads before them ran.

One, as they saw, was shining bright,
With such a great and gracious light,
It seemed that heaven must be in sight.

"This," said the old man, "doth begin
Full sweetly, but its end is in
The dark and desert-place of sin.

"And this, that seemeth all to lie
In gloomy shadow, — by-and-by,
Maketh the gateway of the sky.

"Bide ye a little; fast and pray,
And 'twixt the good and evil way,
Choose ye, my brethren, this day."

And as the day was at the close
The two wayfaring men arose,
And each the road that pleased him chose.

One took the pathway that began
So brightly, and so smoothly ran
Through flowery fields, — deluded man!

Ere long he saw, alas! alas!
All darkly, and as through a glass,
Flames, and not flowers, along the grass.

Then shadows round about him fell,
And in his soul he knew full well
His feet were taking hold on hell.

He tried all vainly to retrace
His pathway; horrors blocked the place,
And demons mocked him to his face.

Broken in spirit, crushed in pride,
One morning by the highway-side
He fell, and all unfriended, died.

The other, after fast and prayer,
Pursued the road that seemed less fair,
And peace went with him, unaware.

And when the old man saw where lay
The traveller's choice, he said, "I pray,
Take this to help you on the way;"

And gave to him a lovely book,
Wherein for guidance he must look,
He told him, if the path should crook.

And so, through labyrinths of shade,
When terror pressed, or doubt dismayed,
He walked in armor all arrayed.

So, over pitfalls travelled he,
And passed the gates of harlotry,
Safe with his heavenly company.

And when the road did low descend,
He found a good inn, and a friend,
And made a comfortable end.

THE BLIND TRAVELLER.

A POOR blind man was travelling one day,
  The guiding staff from out his hand was gone,
And the road crooked, so he lost his way,
  And the night fell, and a great storm came on.

He was not, therefore, troubled and afraid,
  Nor did he vex the silence with his cries,
But on the rainy grass his cheek he laid,
  And waited for the morning sun to rise.

Saying to his heart, — Be still, my heart, and wait,
  For if a good man happen to go by,
He will not leave us to our dark estate
  And the cold cover of the storm, to die;

But he will sweetly take us by the hand,
  And lead us back into the straight highway;
Full soon the clouds will have evanished, and
  All the wide east be blazoned with the day.

And we are like that blind man, all of us, —
Benighted, lost! But while the storm doth fall
Shall we not stay our sinking hearts up, thus, —
Above us there is One who sees it all;

And if His name be Love, as we are told,
He will not leave us to unequal strife;
But to that city with the streets of gold
Bring us, and give us everlasting life.

THE BLACKBIRD.

"I could not think so plain a bird
Could sing so fine a song."

One on another against the wall
Pile up the books, — I am done with them all!
I shall be wise, if I ever am wise,
Out of my own ears, and of my own eyes.

One day of the woods and their balmy light, —
One hour on the top of a breezy hill,
Where in the sassafras all out of sight
The blackbird is splitting his slender bill
For the ease of his heart!
Do you think if he said
I will sing like this bird with the mud-colored back
And the two little spots of gold over his eyes,
Or like to this shy little creature that flies
So low to the ground, with the amethyst rings
About her small throat, — all alive when she sings
With a glitter of shivering green, — for the rest,
Gray shading to gray, with the sheen of her breast
Half rose and half fawn, —

Or like this one so proud,
That flutters so restless, and cries out so loud,
With stiff horny beak and a topknotted head,
And a lining of scarlet laid under his wings,—
Do you think, if he said, "I'm ashamed to be black!"
That he could have shaken the sassafras-tree
As he does with the song he was born to? not he!

MY GOOD ANGEL.

VERY simple are my pleasures, —
  O good angel, stay with me,
  While I number what they be, —
Easy 't is to count my treasures.

Easy 't is, — they are not many:
  Friends for love and company,
  O good angel grant to me;
Strength to work; and is there any

Man or woman, evil seeing
  In my daily walk and way,
  Grant, and give me grace to pray
For a less imperfect being.

Grant a larger light, and better,
  To inform my foe and me,
  So we quickly shall agree;
Grant forgiveness to my debtor.

Make my heart, I pray, of kindness
  Always full, as clouds of showers;
Keep my mortal eyes from blindness;
  I would see the sun and flowers.

From temptation pray deliver;
  And, good angel, grant to me
That my heart be grateful ever:
  Herein all my askings be.

MORE LIFE.

When spring-time prospers in the grass,
  And fills the vales with tender bloom,
And light winds whisper as they pass
  Of sunnier days to come:

In spite of all the joy she brings
  To flood and field, to hill and grove,
This is the song my spirit sings, —
  More light, more life, more love!

And when, her time fulfilled, she goes
  So gently from her vernal place,
And meadow wide and woodland glows
  With sober summer grace:

When on the stalk the ear is set,
  With all the harvest promise bright,
My spirit sings the old song yet, —
  More love, more life, more light!

When stubble takes the place of grain,
  And shrunken streams steal slow along,
And all the faded woods complain
  Like one who suffers wrong;

When fires are lit, and everywhere
  The pleasures of the household rife,
My song is solemnized to prayer, —
  More love, more light, more life!

CONTRADICTORY.

WE contradictory creatures
Have something in us alien to our birth,
That doth suffuse us with the infinite,
While downward through our natures
Run adverse thoughts, that only find delight
In the poor, perishable things of earth.

Blindly we feel about
Our little circle, — ever on the quest
Of knowledge, which is only, at the best,
Pushing the boundaries of our ignorance out.

But while we know all things are miracles,
And that we cannot set
An ear of corn, nor tell a blade of grass
The way to grow, our vanity o'erswells
The limit of our wisdom, and we yet
Audaciously o'erpass
This narrow promontory
Of low, dark land, into the unseen glory,
And with unhallowed zeal
Unto our fellow-men God's judgments deal.

Sometimes along the gloom
We meet a traveller, striking hands with whom,
Maketh a little sweet and tender light
To bless our sight,
And change the clouds around us and above
Into celestial shapes, — and this is love.

Morn cometh, trailing storms,
Even while she wakes a thousand grateful psalms
And with her golden calms
All the wide valley fills;
Darkly they lie below
The purple fire, — the glow,
Where, on the high tops of the eastern hills,
She rests her cloudy arms.

And we are like the morning, — heavenly light
Blowing about our heads, and th' dumb night
Before us and behind us; ceaseless ills
Make up our years; and as from off the hills
The white mists melt, and leave them bare and rough,
So melt from us the fancies of our youth
Until we stand against the last black truth
Naked, and cold, and desolate enough.

THIS IS ALL.

TRYING, trying — always trying —
Falling down to save a fall;
Living by the dint of dying, —
This is all!

Giving, giving — always giving —
Gathering just abroad to cast;
Dying by the dint of living
At the last!

Sighing, smiling — smiling, sighing —
Sun in shade, and shade in sun;
Dying, living — living, dying —
Both in one!

Hoping in our very fearing,
Striving hard against our strife;
Drifting in the stead of steering, —
This is life!

Seeming to believe in seeming,
  Half disproving, to approve;
Knowing that we dream, in dreaming, —
  This is love!

Being in our weakness stronger, —
  Living where there is no breath;
Feeling harm can harm no longer, —
  This is death

IN VAIN.

Down the peach-tree slid
  The milk-white drops of th' dew,
All in that merry time of th' year
  When the world is made anew.

The daisy dressed in white,
  The paw-paw flower in brown,
And th' violet sat by her lover, th' brook,
  With her golden eyelids down.

Gayly its own best hue
  Shone in each leaf and stem, —
Gayly the children rolled on th' grass,
  With their shadows after them.

I said, Be sweet for me,
  O little wild flowers! for I
Have larger need, and shut in myself,
  I wither and waste and die!

Pity me, sing for me!
  I cried to the tuneful bird;
My heart is full of th' spirit of song,
  And I cannot sing a word!

Like a buried stream that longs
  Through th' upper world to run,
And kiss the dawn in her rosy mouth,
  And lie in th' light of th' sun;

So in me, is my soul,
  Wasting in darkness the hours.
Ever fretted and sullen and sad
  With a sense of its unused powers.

In vain! each little flower
  Must be sweet for itself, nor part
With its white or brown, and every bird
  Must sing from its own full heart.

BEST, TO THE BEST.

THE wind blows where it listeth,
  Out of the east and west,
And the sinner's way is as dark as death,
  And life is best, to the best.

The touch of evil corrupteth;
  Tarry not on its track;
The grass where the serpent crawls is stirred
  As if it grew on his back.

To know the beauty of cleanness
  The heart must be clean and sweet;
We must love our neighbor to get his love, —
  As we measure, he will mete.

Cold black crusts to the beggar,
  A cloak of rags and woe;
And the furrows are warm to the sower's feet,
  And his bread is white as snow.

Can blind eyes see the even,
  As he hangs on th' days' soft close,
Like a lusty boy on his mother's neck,
  Bright in the face as a rose?

The grave is cold and cruel, —
  Rest, pregnant with unrest;
And woman must moan and man must groan;
  But life is best, to the best.

THORNS.

I do not think the Providence unkind
  That gives its bad things to this life of ours;
They are the thorns whereby we, travellers blind,
  Feel out our flowers.

I think hate shows the quality of love, —
  That wrong attests that somewhere there is right:
Do not the darkest shadows serve to prove
  The power of light?

On tyrannous ways the feet of Freedom press;
  The green bough broken off, lets sunshine in;
And where sin is, aboundeth righteousness,
  Much more than sin.

Man cannot be all selfish; separate good
  Is nowhere found beneath the shining sun.
All adverse interests, truly understood,
  Resolve to one!

I do believe all worship doth ascend, —
  Whether from temple floors by heathen trod,
Or from the shrines where Christian praises blend, —
  To the true God,

Blessed forever: that His love prepares
  The raven's food; the sparrow's fall doth see;
And, simple, sinful as I am, He cares
  Even for me.

OLD ADAM.

THE wind is blowing cold from the west,
  And your hair is gray and thin;
Come in, old Adam, and shut the door, —
  Come in, old Adam, come in!
"The wind is blowing out o' the west,
  Cold, cold, and my hair is thin;
But it is not there, that face so fair,
  And why should I go in?"

The wind is blowing cold from the west;
  The day is almost gone;
The cock is abed, the cattle fed,
  And the night is coming on!
Come in, old Adam, and shut the door,
  And leave without your care.
"Nay, nay, for the sun of my life is down,
  And the night is everywhere."

The cricket chirps, and your chair is set
  Where the fire shines warm and clear;

Come in, old Adam, and you will forget
  It is not the spring o' the year.
Come in! the wind blows wild from the west,
  And your hair is gray and thin.
"'T is not there now, that sweet, sweet brow,
  And why should I go in?"

THE FARMER'S DAUGHTER.

HER voice was tender as a lullaby,
  Making you think of milk-white dews that creep
Among th' mid-May violets, when they lie,
  All in the yellow moonlight fast asleep.

Ay, tender as that most melodious tone
  The lark has, when within some covert dim
With leaves, he talks with morning all alone,
  Persuading her to rise and come to him.

Shy in her ways; her father's cattle knew—
  No neighbor half so well—her footstep light,
For by the pond where mint and mallows grew
  Always she came and called them home at night

A sad, low pond that cut the field in two
  Wherein they ran, and never billow sent
To play with any breeze, but still withdrew
  Into itself, in wrinkled, dull content.

And here, through mint and mallows she would stray,
  Musing the while she called, as it might be
On th' cold clouds, or winds that with rough gray
  Shingled the landward slope of the near sea.

God knows! not I, on what she mused o' nights
  Straying about the pond: she had no woe
To think upon, they said, nor such delights
  As maids are wont to hide. I only know

We do not know the weakness or the worth
  Of any one: th' Sun as he will may trim
His golden lights; he cannot see the earth
  He loves, but on the side she turns to him.

I only know that when this lonesome pond
  Lifted the buried lilies from its breast
One warm, wet day (I nothing know beyond),
  It lifted her white face up with the rest.

A PRAYER.

I HAVE been little used to frame
Wishes to speech and call it prayer;
To-day, my Father, in Thy name,
I ask to have my soul stript bare
Of all its vain pretence, — to see
Myself, as I am seen by Thee.

I want to know how much the pain
And passion here, its powers abate;
To take its thoughts, a tangled skein,
And stretch them out all smooth and straight;
To track its wavering course through sin
And sorrow, to its origin.

I want to know if in the night
Of evil, grace doth so abound,
That from its darkness we draw light,
As flowers do beauty from the ground;
Or, if the sins of time shall be
The shadows of eternity.

I want, though only for an hour,
  To be myself, — to get more near
The wondrous mystery and power
  Of love, whose echoes floating here,
Between us and the waiting grave,
Make all of light, of heaven, we have.

ALONE.

WHAT shall I do when I stand in my place,
  Unclothed of this garment of cloud and dust,
  Unclothed of this garment of selfish lust,
With my Maker, face to face!

What shall I say for my worldly pride?
  What for the things I have done and *not* done?
  There will be no cloud then over the sun,
And no grave wherein to hide.

No time for waiting, no time for prayer, —
  No friend that with me my life-path trod
  To help me, — only my soul and my God,
And all my sins laid bare.

No dear human pity, no low loving speech,
  About me that terrible day shall there be,
  Remitted back into myself, I shall see
All sweetest things out of reach.

But why should I tremble before th' unknown,
  And put off the blushing and shame? Now, — to-day!
  The friend close beside me seems far, far away,
And I stand at God's judgment alone!

SOMETIMES.

Sometimes for days
Along the fields that I of time have leased,
I go, nor find a single leaf increased;
And hopeless, graze
With forehead stooping downward like a beast.

O heavy hours!
My life seems all a failure, and I sigh,
What is there left for me to do, but die?
So small my powers
That I can only stretch them to a cry!

But while I stretch
What strength I have, though only to a cry,
I gain an utterance that men know me by;
Create, and fetch
A something out of chaos, — that is I.

Good comes to pass
We know not when nor how, for, looking to
What seemed a barren waste, there starts to view
Some bunch of grass,
Or snarl of violets, shining with the dew.

I do believe
The very impotence to pray, is prayer;
The hope that all will end, is in despair,
And while we grieve,
Comfort abideth with us, unaware.

THE SEA-SIDE CAVE.

"A bird of the air shall carry the voice, and that which hath wings tell the matter."

At he dead of night by the side of the Sea
I met my gray-haired enemy, —
The glittering light of his serpent eye
Was all I had to see him by.

At the dead of night, and stormy weather
We went into a cave together, —
Into a cave by the side of the Sea,
And — he never came out with me!

The flower that up through the April mould
Comes like a miser dragging his gold,
Never made spot of earth so bright
As was the ground in the cave that night.

Dead of night, and stormy weather!
Who should see us going together
Under the black and dripping stone
Of the cave from whence I came alone!

Next day as my boy sat on my knee
He picked the gray hairs off from me,
And told with eyes brimful of fear
How a bird in the meadow near

Over her clay-built nest had spread
Sticks and leaves all bloody red,
Brought from a cave by the side of the Sea
Where some murdered man must be.

JANUARY.

The year has lost its leaves again,
  The world looks old and grim;
God folds his robe of glory thus,
  That we may see but Him.

And all his stormy messengers,
  That come with whirlwind breath,
Beat out our chaff of vanity,
  And leave the grains of faith.

We will not feel, while summer waits
  Her rich delights to share,
What sinners, miserably bad, —
  How weak and poor we are.

We tread through fields of speckled flowers
  As if we did not know
Our Father made them beautiful,
  Because He loves us so.

We hold his splendors in our hands
  As if we held the dust,
And deal his judgment, as if man
  Than God could be more just.

We seek, in prayers and penances,
  To do the martyr's part,
Remembering not, the promises
  Are to the pure in heart.

From evil and forbidden things,
  Some good we think to win,
And to the last analysis
  Experiment with sin.

We seek no oil in summer time
  Our winter lamp to trim,
But strive to bring God down to us,
  More than to rise to Him.

And when that He is nearest, most
  Our weak complaints we raise,
Lacking the wisdom to perceive
  The mystery of his ways.

For, when drawn closest to himself,
  Then least his love we mark;
The very wings that shelter us
  From peril, make it dark.

Sometimes He takes his hands from us,
  When storms the loudest blow,
That we may learn how weak, alone,—
  How strong in Him, we grow.

Through the cross iron of our free will
And fate, we plead for light,
As if God gave us not enough
To do our work aright.

We will not see, but madly take
The wrong and crooked path,
And in our own hearts light the fires
Of a consuming wrath.

The fashion of his Providence
Our way is so above,
We serve Him most who take the most
Of his exhaustless love.

We serve Him in the good we do,
The blessings we embrace,
Not lighting farthing candles for
The palace of his grace.

He has no need of our poor aid
His purpose to pursue;
'T is for our pleasure, not for his,
That we his work must do.

Then blow, O wild winds, as ye list,
And let the world look grim, —
God folds his robe of glory thus
That we may see but Him.

THE MEASURE OF TIME.

A BREATH, like the wind's breath, may carry
  A name far and wide,
But the measure of time does not tally
  With any man's pride.

'T is not a wild chorus of praises,
  Nor chance, nor yet fate, —
'T is the greatness born with him, and in him,
  That makes the man great.

And when in the calm self-possession
  That birthright confers,
The man is stretched out to her measure,
  Fame claims him for hers.

Too proud to fall back on achievement,
  With work in his sight,
His triumph may not overtake him
  This side of the night.

And men, with his honors about them,
  His grave-mound may pass,
Nor dream what a great heart lies under
  Its short knotty grass.

But though he has lived thus unprospered,
And died thus, alone,
His face may not always be hid by
A handbreadth of stone.

The long years are wiser than any
Wise day of them all,
And the hero at last shall stand upright, —
The base image fall.

The counterfeit may for a season
Deceive the wide earth,
But the lie, waxing great, comes to labor,
And truth has its birth.

IDLE FEARS.

In my lost childhood old folks said to me,
"Now is the time and season of your bliss;
All joy is in the hope of joy to be,
Not in possession; and in after years
You will look back with longing sighs and tears
To the young days when you from care were free."
It was not true; they nurtured idle fears;
I never saw so good a day as this!

And youth and I have parted: long ago
I looked into my glass, and saw one day
A little silver line that told me so:
At first I shut my eyes and cried, and then
I hid it under girlish flowers, but when
Persuasion would not make my mate to stay,
I bowed my faded head, and said, "Amen!"
And all my peace is since she went away.

My window opens toward the autumn woods;
I see the ghosts of thistles walk the air
O'er the long, level stubble-land that broods;
Beneath the herbless rocks that jutting lie,

Summer has gathered her white family
Of shrinking daisies; all the hills are bare,
And in the meadows not a limb of buds
Through the brown bushes showeth anywhere.

Dear, beauteous season, we must say good-bye,
And can afford to, we have been so blest,
And farewells suit the time; the year doth lie
With cloudy skirts composed, and pallid face
Hid under yellow leaves, with touching grace,
So that her bright-haired sweetheart of the sky
The image of her prime may not displace.

HINTS.

Two thirsty travellers chanced one day to meet
  Where a spring bubbled from the burning sand ;
  One drank out of the hollow of his hand,
And found the water very cool and sweet.

The other waited for a smith to beat
  And fashion for his use a golden cup ;
And while he waited, fainting in the heat,
  The sunshine came and drank the fountain up !

In a green field two little flowers there were,
  And both were fair in th' face and tender-eyed ;
  One took the light and dew that heaven supplied,
And all the summer gusts were sweet with her.

The other, to her nature false, denied
  That she had any need of sun and dew,
  And hung her silly head, and sickly grew,
And frayed and faded, all untimely died.

A vine o' th' bean, that had been early wed
  To a tall peach, conceiving that he hid
  Her glories from the world, unwisely slid
Out of his arms, and vainly chafing, said:

"This fellow is an enemy of mine,
  And dwarfs me with his shade": she would not see
  That she was made a vine, and not a tree,
And that a tree is stronger tnan a vine.

TO A STAGNANT RIVER.

O river, why lie with your beautiful face
To the hill? Can you move him away from his place?
You may moan, — you may clasp him with soft arms forever, —
He will still be a flinty hill, — you be a river.

'T is wilful, 't is wicked to waste in despair
The treasure so many are dying to share,
The gifts that we have, Heaven lends for right using,
And not for ignoring, and not for abusing.

Let the moss have his love, and the grass and the dew, —
By God's law he cannot be mated with you.
His friend is the stubble, his life is the dust,
You are not what you would, — you must be what you must.

If into his keeping your fortune you cast,
I tell you the end will be hatred at last,
Or death through stagnation; your rest is in motion;
The aim of your being, the cloud and the ocean.

Love cannot be love, with itself set at strife;
To sin against Nature is death and not life.
You may freeze in the shadow or seethe in the sun,
But the oil and the water will not be at one.

Your pride and your peace, when this passion is crossed
Will pay for the struggle whatever it cost;
But though earth dissolve, though the heavens should fall,
To yourself, your Creator, be true first of all.

COUNSEL.

SEEK not to walk by borrowed light,
  But keep unto thine own:
Do what thou doest with thy might,
  And trust thyself alone!

Work for some good, nor idly lie
  Within the human hive;
And, though the outward man should die,
  Keep thou the heart alive!

Strive not to banish pain and doubt,
  In pleasure's noisy din;
The peace thou seekest for without
  Is only found within.

If fortune disregard thy claim,
  By worth, her slight attest;
Nor blush and hang the head for shame
  When thou hast done thy best.

What thy experience teaches true,
  Be vigilant to heed;
The wisdom that we suffer to,
  Is wiser than a creed.

Disdain neglect, ignore despair,
  On loves and friendships gone
Plant thou thy feet, as on a stair,
  And mount right up and on!

LATENT LIFE.

THOUGH never shown by word or deed,
  Within us lies some germ of power,
As lies unguessed, within the seed,
  The latent flower.

And under every common sense
  That doth its daily use fulfil,
There lies another, more intense,
  And beauteous still.

This dusty house, wherein is shrined
  The soul, is but the counterfeit
Of that which shall be, more refined,
  And exquisite.

The light which to our sight belongs,
  Enfolds a light more broad and clear;
Music but intimates the songs
  We do not hear.

The fond embrace, the tender kiss
  Which love to its expression brings,
Are but the husk the chrysalis
  Wears on its wings.

The vigor falling to decay,
  Hopes, impulses that fade and die,
Are but the layers peeled away
  From life more high.

When death shall come and disallow
  These rough and ugly masks we wear,
I think that we shall be as now, —
  Only more fair.

And He who makes his love to be
  Always around me, sure and calm,
Sees what is possible to me,
  Not what I am.

HOW AND WHERE.

How are we living?
Like herbs in a garden that stand in a row,
And have nothing to do but to stand there and grow?
Our powers of perceiving
So dull and so dead,
They simply extend to the objects about us, —
The moth, having all his dark pleasure without us, —
The worm in his bed!

If thus we are living,
And fading, and falling, and rotting, alas! —
Like the grass, or the flowers that grow in the grass, —
Is life worth our having?
The insect a-humming, —
The wild bird is better, that sings as it flies, —
The ox, that turns up his great face to the skies,
When the thunder is coming.

Where are we living?
In passion, and pain, and remorse do we dwell, —
Creating, yet terribly hating, our hell?
No triumph achieving?

No grossness refining?
The wild tree does more; for his coat of rough barks
He trims with green mosses, and checks with the marks
Of the long summer shining.

We 're dying, not living:
Our senses shut up, and our hearts faint and cold;
Upholding old things just because they are old;
Our good spirits grieving,
We suffer our springs
Of promise to pass without sowing the land,
And hungry and sad in the harvest-time stand,
Expecting good things!

THE FELLED TREE.

THEY set me up, and bade me stand
  Beside a dark, dark sea,
In the befogged, low-lying land,
  Of this mortality.

I slipped my roots round the stony soil
  Like rings on the hand of a bride,
And my boughs took hold of the summer's smile
  And grew out green and wide.

Crooked, and shaggy on all sides,
  I was homeliest of trees,
But the cattle rubbed their speckled hides
  Against my knotty knees;

And lambs, in white rows on the grass,
  Lay down within my shade;
So I knew, all homely as I was,
  For a good use I was made.

And my contentment served me well;
  My heart grew strong and sweet,
And my shaggy bark cracked off and fell
  In layers at my feet.

I felt when the darkest storm was rife
  The day of its wrath was brief,
And that I drew from the centre of life
  The life of my smallest leaf.

At last a woodman came one day
  With axe to a sharp edge ground,
And hewed at my heart till I stood a-sway,
  But I never felt the wound.

I knew immortal seed was sown
  Within me at my birth,
And I fell without a single groan,
  With my green face to the earth.

Now all men pity me, and must,
  Who see me lie so low,
But the Power that changes me to dust
  Is the same that made me grow.

A DREAM.

I DREAMED I had a plot of ground,
Once when I chanced asleep to drop,
And that a green hedge fenced it round,
Cloudy with roses at the top.

I saw a hundred mornings rise, —
So far a little dream may reach, —
And Spring with Summer in her eyes
Making the chiefest charm of each.

A thousand vines were climbing o'er
The hedge, I thought, but as I tried
To pull them down, forevermore
The flowers dropt off the other side!

Waking, I said, these things are signs
Sent to instruct us that 't is ours
Duly to keep and dress our vines, —
Waiting in patience for the flowers.

And when the angel feared of all
Across my hearth its shadow spread,
The rose that climbed my garden wall
Has bloomed the other side, I said.

WORK.

Down and up, and up and down,
  Over and over and over;
Turn in the little seed, dry and brown,
  Turn out the bright red clover.
Work, and the sun your work will share,
  And the rain in its time will fall;
For Nature, she worketh everywhere,
  And the grace of God through all.

With hand on the spade and heart in the sky,
  Dress the ground, and till it;
Turn in the little seed, brown and dry,
  Turn out the golden millet.
Work, and your house shall be duly fed;
  Work, and rest shall be won;
I hold that a man had better be dead
  Than alive, when his work is done!

Down and up, and up and down,
  On the hill-top, low in the valley;
Turn in the little seed, dry and brown,
  Turn out the rose and lily.

Work with a plan, or without a plan,
  And your ends they shall be shaped true;
Work, and learn at first hand, like a man, —
  The best way to *know*, is to *do!*

Down and up till life shall close,
  Ceasing not your praises;
Turn in the wild white winter snows,
  Turn out the sweet spring daisies.
Work, and the sun your work will share,
  And the rain in its time will fall;
For Nature, she worketh everywhere,
  And the grace of God through all.

COMFORT.

Boatman, boatman! my brain is wild,
  As wild as the stormy seas;
My poor little child, my sweet little child,
  Is a corpse upon my knees.

No holy choir to sing so low,
  No priest to kneel in prayer,
No tire-woman to help me sew
  A cap for his golden hair.

Dropping his oars in the rainy sea,
  The pious boatman cried,
Not without Him who is life to thee
  Could the little child have died!

His grace the same, and the same His power,
  Demanding our love and trust,
Whether He makes of the dust a flower,
  Or changes a flower to dust.

On the land and the water, all in all,
  The strength to be still or pray,
To blight the leaves in their time to fall,
  Or light up the hills with May.

FAITH AND WORKS.

NOT what we think, but what we *do*,
  Makes saints of us: all stiff and cold,
The outlines of the corpse show through
  The cloth of gold.

And in despite the outward sin, —
  Despite belief with creeds at strife, —
The principle of love within
  Leavens the life.

For, 't is for fancied good, I claim,
  That men do wrong, — not wrong's desire;
Wrapping themselves, as 't were, in flame
  To cheat the fire.

Not what God gives, but what He takes,
  Uplifts us to the holiest height;
On truth's rough crags life's current breaks
  To diamond light.

From transient evil I do trust
  That we a final good shall draw;
That in confusion, death, and dust,
  Are light and law.

That He whose glory shines among
  The eternal stars, descends to mark
This foolish little atom swung
  Loose in the dark.

But though I should not thus receive
  A sense of order and control,
My God, I could not disbelieve
  My sense of soul.

For though, alas! I can but see
  A hand's breadth backward, or before,
I *am*, and since I am, must be
  Forevermore.

THE RUSTIC PAINTER.

His sheep went idly over the hills, —
  Idly down and up, —
As he sat and painted his sweetheart's face
  On a little ivory cup.

All round him roses lay in the grass
  That were hardly out of buds;
For sake of her mouth and cheek, I knew
  He had murdered them in the woods.

The ant, that good little housekeeper,
  Was not at work so hard;
And yet the semblance of a smile
  Was all of his reward:

And the golden-belted gentleman
  That travels in the air,
Hummed not so sweet to the clover-buds
  As he to his picture there.

The while for his ivory cup he made
  An easel of his knee,
And painted his little sweetheart's face
  Truly and tenderly.

Thus we are marking on all our work
  Whatever we have of grace;
As the rustic painted his ivory cup
  With his little sweetheart's face.

ONE OF MANY.

I KNEW a man — I know him still
  In part, in all I ever knew, —
Whose life runs counter to his will,
  Leaving the things he fain would do,

Undone. His hopes are shapes of sands,
  That cannot with themselves agree;
As one whose eager, outstretched hands
  Take hold on water — so is he.

Fame is a bauble, to his ken;
  Mirth cannot move his aspect grim;
The holidays of other men
  Are only battle-days to him.

He locks his heart within his breast,
  Believing life to such as he
Is but a change of ills, at best, —
  A crossed and crazy tragedy.

His cheek is wan; his limbs are faint
  With fetters which they never wore;
No wheel that ever crushed a saint,
  But breaks *his* body o'er and o'er.

Though woman's grace he never sought
  By tender look, or word of praise,
He dwells upon her in his thought,
  With all a lover's lingering phrase.

A very martyr to the truth,
  All that 's best in him is belied;
Humble, yet proud withal; in sooth
  His pride is his disdain of pride.

He sees in what he does amiss
  A continuity of ill;
The next life dropping out of this,
  Stained with its many colors still.

His kindliest pity is for those
  Who are the slaves of guilty lusts;
And virtue, shining till it shows
  Another's frailty, he distrusts.

Nature, he holds, since time began
  Has been reviled, — misunderstood;
And that we first must love a man
  To judge him, — be he bad or good.

Often his path is crook'd and low,
  And is so in his own despite;
For still the path he meant to go
  Runs straight, and level with the right.

No heart has he to strive with fate
  For less things than our great men gone
Achieved, who, with their single weight,
  Turned time's slow wheels a century on.

His waiting silence is his prayer;
  His darkness is his plea for light;
And loving all men everywhere,
  He lives, a more than anchorite.

O friends, if you this man should see,
  Be not your scorn too hardly hurled,
Believe me, whatsoe'er he be,
  There be more like him in the world.

THE SHADOW.

ONE summer night,
The full moon, 'tired in her golden cloak,
Did beckon me, I thought; and I awoke,
And saw a light,

Most soft and fair,
Shine in the brook, as if, in love's distress,
The parting sun had shear'd a dazzling tress,
And left it there.

Toward the sweet banks
Of the bright stream straightly I bent my way;
And in my heart good thoughts the while did stay,
Giving God thanks.

The wheat-stocks stood
Along the field like little fairy men,
And mists stole, white and bashful, through the glen,
As maidens would.

In rich content
My soul was growing toward immortal height,
When, lo! I saw that by me, through the light,
A shadow went.

I stopped, afraid:
It was the bad sign of some evil done;
That stopping, too, right swiftly did I run;
So did the shade.

At length I drew
Close to the bank of the delightful brook,
And sitting in the moonshine, turn'd to look;
It sat there too.

Ere long I spied
A weed with goodly flowers upon its top;
And when I saw that such sweet things did drop
Black shadows, cried,—

Lo! I have found,
Hid in this ugly riddle, a good sign;
My life is twofold, earthly and divine,—
Buried and crown'd.

Sown darkly; raised
Light within light, when death from mortal soil
Undresses me, and makes me spiritual:—
Dear Lord, be praised.

THE UNWISE CHOICE.

Two young men, when I was poor,
Came and stood at my open door;

One said to me, "I have gold to give;"
And one, "I will love you while I live!"

My sight was dazzled; woe 's the day!
And I sent the poor young man away;

Sent him away, I know not where,
And my heart went with him, unaware.

He did not give me any sighs,
But he left his picture in my eyes;

And in my eyes it has always been:
I have no heart to keep it in!

Beside the lane with hedges sweet,
Where we parted, never more to meet,

He pulled a flower of love's own hue,
And where it had been came out two!

And in th' grass where he stood, for years,
The dews of th' morning looked like tears.

Still smiles the house where I was born
Among its fields of wheat and corn.

Wheat and corn that strangers bind, —
I reap as I sowed, and I sowed to th' wind.

As one who feels the truth break through
His dream, and knows his dream untrue,

I live where splendors shine, and sigh,
For the peace that splendor cannot buy;

Sigh for the day I was rich tho' poor,
And saw th' two young men at my door!

SIGNS OF GRACE.

Come thou, my heavy soul, and lay
  Thy sorrows all aside,
And let us see, if so we may,
  How God is glorified.

Forget the storms that darkly beat,
  Forget the woe and crime,
And tie of consolations sweet
  A posie for the time.

Some blessed token everywhere
  Doth grace to men allow;
The daisy sets her silver share
  Beside the rustic's plough.

The wintry wind that naked strips
  The bushes, stoopeth low,
And round their rugged arms enwraps
  The fleeces of the snow.

The blackbird, idly whistling till
  The storm begins to pour,
Finds ever with his golden bill
  A hospitable door.

From love, and love's protecting power
 We cannot go apart;
The shadows round the fainting flower
 Rebuke the drooping heart.

Our strivings are not reckoned less,
 Although we fail to win;
The lily wears a royal dress,
 And yet she doth not spin.

So, Soul, forget thy evil days,
 Thy sorrow lay aside,
And strive to see in all His ways
 How God is glorified.

PROVIDENCE.

"From seeming evil, still educing good."

The stone upon the wayside seed that fell,
  And kept the spring rain from it, kept it too
From the bird's mouth; and in that silent cell
  It quickened, after many days, and grew,
Till, by-and-by, a rose, a single one,
Lifted its little face into the sun.

It chanced a wicked man approached one day,
  And saw the tender, piteous look it wore:
Perhaps one like it somewhere far away
  Grew in a garden-bed, or by the door
That he in childish days had played around,
For his knees, trembling, sunk upon the ground.

Then, o'er this piece of bleeding earth, the tears
  Of penitence were wrung, until at last
The golden key of love, that sin for years
  In his unquiet soul had rusted fast,
Was loosened, and his heart, that very hour,
Opened to God's good sunshine, like a flower.

THE LIVING PRESENT.

FRIENDS, let us slight no pleasant spring
That bubbles up in life's dry sands,
And yet be careful what good thing
We touch with sacrilegious hands.

Our blessings should be *sought*, not *claimed*, —
Cherished, not watched with jealous eye;
Love is too precious to be named,
Save with a reverence deep and high.

In all that lives, exists the power
To avenge the invasion of its right;
We cannot bruise and break our flower,
And have our flower, alive and bright.

Let us think less of what appears, —
More of what *is;* for this, hold I,
It is the sentence no man hears
That makes us live, or makes us die.

Trust hearsay less; seek more to prove
  And know if things be what they seem;
Not sink supinely in some groove,
  And hope and hope, and dream and dream.

Some days must needs be full of gloom,
  Yet must we use them as we may;
Talk less about the years to come, —
  Live, love, and labor more, to-day.

What our hand findeth, do with might;
  Ask less for help, but stand or fall,
Each one of us, in life's great fight,
  As if himself and God were all.

ONE DUST.

Thou, under Satan's fierce control,
  Shall Heaven its final rest bestow?
I know not, but I know a soul
  That might have fallen as darkly low.

I judge thee not, what depths of ill
  Soe'er thy feet have found, or trod;
I know a spirit and a will
  As weak, but for the grace of God.

Shalt thou with full-day laborers stand,
  Who hardly canst have pruned one vine?
I know not, but I know a hand
  With an infirmity like thine.

Shalt thou who hast with scoffers part,
  E'er wear the crown the Christian wears?
I know not, but I know a heart
  As flinty, but for tears and prayers.

Have mercy, O Thou Crucified!
  For even while I name Thy name,
I know a tongue that might have lied
  Like Peter's, and am bowed with shame.

Fighters of good fights, — just, unjust, —
  The weak who faint, the frail who fall, —
Of one blood, of the self-same dust,
  Thou, God of love, hast made them all.

THE WEAVER'S DREAM.

He sat all alone in his dark little room,
His fingers aweary with work at the loom,
His eyes seeing not the fine threads, for the tears,
As he carefully counted the months and the years
He had been a poor weaver.

Not a traveller went on the dusty highway,
But he thought, "He has nothing to do but be gay;"
No matter how burdened or bent he might be,
The weaver believed him more happy than he,
And sighed at his weaving.

He saw not the roses so sweet and so red
That looked through his window; he thought to be dead

And carried away from his dark little room,
Wrapt up in the linen he had in his loom,
    Were better than weaving.

Just then a white angel came out of the skies,
And shut up his senses, and sealed up his eyes,
And bore him away from the work at his loom
In a vision, and left him alone by the tomb
    Of his dear little daughter.

"My darling!" he cries, "what a blessing was mine!
How I sinned, having you, against goodness divine!
Awake! O my lost one, my sweet one, awake!
And I never, as long as I live, for your sake,
    Will sigh at my weaving!"

The sunset was gilding his low little room
When the weaver awoke from his dream at the loom,
And close at his knee saw a dear little head
Alight with long curls, — she was living, not dead, —
    His pride and his treasure.

He winds the fine thread on his shuttle anew,
(At thought of his blessing 't was easy to do,)
And sings as he weaves, for the joy in his breast,
Peace cometh of striving, and labor is rest:
    Grown wise was the weaver.

NOT NOW.

THE path of duty I clearly trace,
I stand with conscience face to face,
  And all her pleas allow;
Calling and crying the while for grace, —
"Some other time, and some other place:
  O, not to-day; not now!"

I know 't is a demon boding ill,
I know I have power to do if I will,
  And I put my hand to th' plough;
I have fair, sweet seeds in my barn, and lo!
When all the furrows are ready to sow,
  The voice says, "O, not now!"

My peace I sell at the price of woe;
In heart and in spirit I suffer so,
  The anguish wrings my brow;
But still I linger and cry for grace, —
"Some other time, and some other place:
  O, not to-day; not now!"

I talk to my stubborn heart and say,
The work I must do I will do to-day;
I will make to the Lord a vow:
And I will not rest and I will not sleep
Till the vow I have vowed I rise and keep;
And the demon cries, "Not now!"

And so the days and the years go by,
And so I register lie upon lie,
And break with Heaven my vow;
For when I would boldly take my stand,
This terrible demon stays my hand, —
"O, not to-day: not now!"

CRAGS.

THERE was a good and reverend man
  Whose day of life, serene and bright,
Was wearing hard upon the gloom
  Beyond which we can see no light.

And as his vision back to morn,
  And forward to the evening sped,
He bowed himself upon his staff,
  And with his heart communing, said:

From mystery on to mystery
  My way has been; yet as I near
The eternal shore, against the sky
  These crags of truth stand sharp and clear.

Where'er its hidden fountain be,
  Time is a many-colored jet
Of good and evil, light and shade,
  And we evoke the things we get.

The hues that our to-morrows wear
  Are by our yesterdays forecast;
Our future takes into itself
  The true impression of our past.

The attrition of conflicting thoughts
  To clear conclusions, wears the groove;
The love that seems to die, dies not,
  But is absorbed in larger love.

We cannot cramp ourselves, unharmed,
  In bonds of iron, nor of creeds;
The rights that rightfully belong
  To man, are measured by his needs.

The daisy is entitled to
  The nurture of the dew and light;
The green house of the grasshopper
  Is his by Nature's sacred right.

MAN.

In what a kingly fashion man doth dwell:
    He hath but to prefer
    His want, and Nature, like a servitor,
Maketh him answer with some miracle.

And yet his thoughts do keep along the ground,
    And neither leap nor run,
    Though capable to climb above the sun;
He seemeth free, and yet is strangely bound.

What name would suit his case, or great or small?
    Poor, but exceeding proud;
    Importunate and still, humble and loud;
Most wise, and yet most ignorant, withal.

The world that lieth in the golden air,
    Like a great emerald,
    Knoweth the law by which she is upheld,
And in her motions keepeth steady there.

But in his foolishness proud man defies
The law, wherewith is bound
The peace he seeks, and fluttering moth-like round
Some dangerous light, experimenting, dies.

And all his subtle reasoning can obtain
To tell his fortune by,
Is only that he liveth and must die,
And dieth in the hope to live again.

TO SOLITUDE.

I AM weary of the working,
  Weary of the long day's heat;
To thy comfortable bosom,
  Wilt thou take me, spirit sweet?

Weary of the long, blind struggle
  For a pathway bright and high, —
Weary of the dimly dying
  Hopes that never quite all die.

Weary searching a bad cipher
  For a good that must be meant;
Discontent with being weary, —
  Weary with my discontent.

I am weary of the trusting
  Where my trusts but torments prove;
Wilt thou keep faith with me? wilt thou
  Be my true and tender love?

I am weary drifting, driving
  Like a helmless bark at sea;
Kindly, comfortable spirit,
  Wilt thou give thyself to me?

Give thy birds to sing me sonnets?
  Give thy winds my cheeks to kiss?
And thy mossy rocks to stand for
  The memorials of our bliss?

I in reverence will hold thee,
  Never vexed with jealous ills,
Though thy wild and wimpling waters
  Wind about a thousand hills.

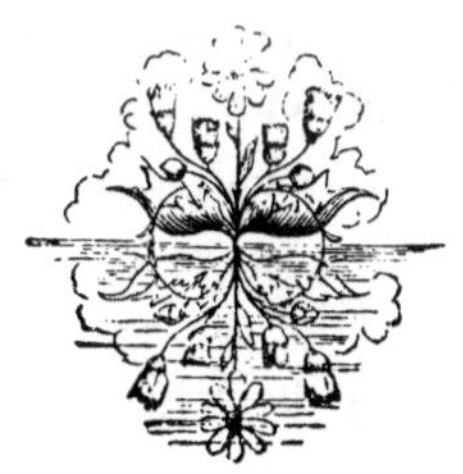

THE LAW OF LIBERTY.

This extent hath freedom's ground, —
In my freedom I am bound
Never any soul to wound.

Not my own: it is not mine,
Lord, except to make it thine,
By good works through grace divine.

Not another's: Thou alone
Keepest judgment for thine own;
Only unto Thee is known

What to pity, what to blame;
How the fierce temptation came:
What is honor, what is shame.

Right is bound in this — to win
Good till injury begin;
That, and only that, is sin.

Selfish good may not befall
Any man, or great or small;
Best for one is best for all.

And who vainly doth desire
Good through evil to acquire,
In his bosom taketh fire.

Wronging no man, Lord, nor Thee
Vexing, I do pray to be
In my soul, my body, free.

Free to freely leave behind
When the better things I find,
Worser things, howe'er enshrined.

So that pain may peace enhance,
And through every change and chance,
I upon myself, advance.

MY CREED.

I HOLD that Christian grace abounds
  Where charity is seen; that when
We climb to Heaven, 't is on the rounds
  Of love to men.

I hold all else, named piety,
  A selfish scheme, a vain pretence;
Where centre is not — can there be
  Circumference?

This I moreover hold, and dare
  Affirm where'er my rhyme may go, —
Whatever things be sweet or fair,
  Love makes them so.

Whether it be the lullabies
  That charm to rest the nursling bird,
Or that sweet confidence of sighs
  And blushes, made without a word.

Whether the dazzling and the flush
  Of softly sumptuous garden bowers,
Or by some cabin door, a bush
  Of ragged flowers.

'T is not the wide phylactery,
  Nor stubborn fast, nor stated prayers,
That make us saints: we judge the tree
  By what it bears.

And when a man can live apart
  From works, on theologic trust,
I know the blood about his heart
  Is dry as dust.

OPEN SECRETS.

THE truth lies round about us, all
  Too closely to be sought, —
So open to our vision that
  'T is hidden to our thought.

We know not what the glories
  Of the grass, the flower, may be;
We needs must struggle for the sight
  Of what we always see.

Waiting for storms and whirlwinds,
  And to have a sign appear,
We deem not God is speaking in
  The still small voice we hear.

In reasoning proud, blind leaders of
  The blind, through life we go,
And do not know the things we see,
  Nor see the things we know.

Single and indivisible,
  We pass from change to change,
Familiar with the strangest things,
  And with familiar, strange.

We make the light through which we see
  The light, and make the dark;
To hear the lark sing, we must be
  At heaven's gate with the lark.

THE SADDEST SIGHT.

As one that leadeth a blind man
  In a city, to and fro,
  Thought, even so,
Leadeth me still wherever it will
  Through scenes of joy and woe.

I have seen Lear, his white head crowned
  With poor straws, playing King;
  And, wearying
Her cheeks' young flowers "with true-love showers,'
  I have heard Ophelia sing.

I have been in battles, and I have seen
  Stones at the martyrs hurled, —
  Seen th' flames curled
Round foreheads bold, and lips whence rolled
  The litanies of the world.

But of all sad sights that ever I saw,
  The saddest under the sun,
  Is a little one,
Whose poor pale face was despoiled of grace
  Ere yet its life begun.

No glimpse of the good green Nature
  To gladden with sweet surprise
  The staring eyes,
That only have seen, close walls between,
  A hand-breadth of the skies.

Ah, never a bird is heard to sing
  At the windows under ground,
  The long year round;
There, never the morn on her pipes of corn
  Maketh a cheerful sound.

Oh, little white cloud of witnesses
  Against your parentage,
  May Heaven assuage
The woes that wait on your dark estate,—
  Unorphaned orphanage.

THE BRIDAL HOUR.

"THE moon's gray tent is up: another hour,
  And yet another one will bring the time
To which, through many cares and checks, so slowly,
  The golden day did climb.

"Take all the books away, and let no noises
  Be in the house while softly I undress
My soul from broideries of disguise, and wait for
  My own true love's caress.

"The sweetest sound would tire to-night; the dewdrops
  Setting the green ears in the corn and wheat,
Would make a discord in the heart attuned to
  The bridegroom's coming feet.

"Love! blessed Love! if we could hang our walls with
  The splendors of a thousand rosy Mays,
Surely they would not shine so well as thou dost,
  Lighting our dusty days.

"Without thee, what a dim and woful story
  Our years would be, oh, excellence sublime!
Slip of the life eternal, brightly growing
  In the low soil of time!"

IDLE.

I HEARD the gay spring coming,
I saw the clover blooming,
  Red and white along the meadows, —
  Red and white along the streams;
I heard the bluebird singing,
I saw the green grass springing,
  All as I lay a-dreaming, —
  A-dreaming idle dreams.

I heard the ploughman's whistle,
I saw the rough burr thistle
  In the sharp teeth of the harrow, —
  Saw the summer's yellow gleams
In the walnuts, in the fennel,
In the mulleins, lined with flannel,
  All as I lay a-dreaming, —
  A-dreaming idle dreams.

I felt the warm, bright weather;
Saw the harvest, — saw them gather
  Corn and millet, wheat and apples, —
  Saw the gray barns with their seams

Pressing wide, — the bare-armed shearers, —
The ruddy water-bearers, —
All as I lay a-dreaming, —
A-dreaming idle dreams.

The bluebird and her nestling
Flew away; the leaves fell rustling,
The cold rain killed the roses,
The sun withdrew his beams;
No creature cared about me,
The world could do without me,
All as I lay a-dreaming, —
A-dreaming idle dreams.

Hymns.

THE SURE WITNESS.

THE solemn wood had spread
Shadows around my head, —
" Curtains they are," I said,
" Hung dim and still about the house of prayer ; "
Softly among the limbs,
Turning the leaves of hymns,
I heard the winds, and asked if God were there.
No voice replied, but while I listening stood,
Sweet peace made holy hushes through the wood.

With ruddy, open hand,
I saw the wild rose stand
Beside the green gate of the summer hills,
And pulling at her dress,
I cried, " Sweet hermitess,
Hast thou beheld Him who the dew distils ? "
No voice replied, but while I listening bent,
Her gracious beauty made my heart content.

The moon in splendor shone, —
"She walketh Heaven alone,
And seeth all things," to myself I mused;
"Hast thou beheld Him, then,
Who hides himself from men
In that great power through Nature interfused?"
No speech made answer, and no sign appeared,
But in the silence I was soothed and cheered.

Waking one time, strange awe
Thrilling my soul, I saw
A kingly splendor round about the night;
Such cunning work the hand
Of spinner never planned, —
The finest wool may not be washed so white.
"Hast thou come out of Heaven?" I asked; and lo
The snow was all the answer of the snow.

Then my heart said, "Give o'er;
Question no more, no more!
The wind, the snow-storm, the wild hermit flower,
The illuminated air,
The pleasure after prayer,
Proclaim the unoriginated Power!
The mystery that hides Him here and there,
Bears the sure witness He is everywhere."

LOVE IS LIFE.

Our days are few and full of strife;
  Like leaves our pleasures fade and fall;
  But Thou who art the all in all,
Thy name is Love, and love is Life!

We walk in sleep and think we see;
  Our little lives are clothed with dreams;
  For that to us which substance seems
Is shadow, 'twixt ourselves and Thee.

We are immortal now, and here,
  Chances and changes, night and day,
  Are landmarks in the eternal way;
Our fear is all we have to fear.

Our lives are dew-drops in Thy sun;
  Thou breakest them, and lo! we see
  A thousand gracious shapes of Thee,—
A thousand shapes, instead of one.

The soul that drifts all darkly dim
  Through floods that seem outside of grace,
  Is only surging toward the place
Which Thou hast made and meant for him.

For this we hold, — ill could not be
Were there no power beyond the ill;
Our wills are held within Thy will;
The ends of goodness rest with Thee.

Fall storms of winter as you may,
The dry boughs in the warm spring rain
Shall put their green leaves forth again,
And surely we are more than they.

THY works, O Lord, interpret Thee,
And through them all Thy love is shown;
Flowing about us like a sea,
Yet steadfast as the eternal throne.

Out of the light that runneth through
Thy hand, the lily's dress is spun;
Thine is the brightness of the dew,
And thine the glory of the sun.

TIME.

WHAT is time, O, glorious Giver,
 With its restlessness and might,
But a lost and wandering river
 Working back into the light?

Every gloomy rock that troubles
 Its smooth passage, strikes to life
Beautiful and joyous bubbles
 That are only born through strife.

Overhung with mist-like shadows,
 Stretch its shores away, away,
To the long, delightful meadows
 Shining with immortal May:

Where its moaning reaches never,
 Passion, pain, or fear to move,
And the changes bring us ever
 Sabbaths and new moons of love.

CONSOLATION.

O friends, we are drawing nearer home
As day by day goes by;
Nearer the fields of fadeless bloom,
The joys that never die.

Ye doubting souls, from doubt be free,—
Ye mourners, mourn no more,
For every wave of Death's dark sea
Breaks on that blissful shore.

God's ways are high above our ways,—
So shall we learn at length,
And tune our lives to sing His praise
With all our mind, might, strength.

About our devious paths of ill
He sets His stern decrees,
And works the wonders of His will
Through pains and promises.

Strange are the mysteries He employs,
Yet we His love will trust,
Though it should blight our dearest joys,
And bruise us into dust.

SUPPLICATION.

O Thou, who all my life hast crowned
  With better things than I could ask,
  Be it to-day my humble task
To own from depths of grief profound,
  The many sins, which darken through
  What little good I do.

I have been too much used, I own,
  To tell my needs in fretful words;
  The clamoring of the silly birds,
Impatient till their wings be grown,
  Have Thy forgiveness. O, my blessed Lord,
  The like to me accord.

Of grace, as much as will complete
  Thy will in me, I pray Thee for;
  Even as a rose shut in a drawer
That maketh all about it sweet,
  I would be, rather than the cedar fine:
  Help me, thou Power divine.

With charity fill Thou my heart,
  As Summer fills the grass with dews,

And as th' year itself renews
In th' sun, when Winter days depart,
'Blessed forever, grant Thou me
To be renewed in Thee.

Why should our spirits be opprest
When days of darkness fall?
Our Father knoweth what is best,
And He hath made them all.

He made them, and to all their length
Set parallels of gain;
We gather from our pain the strength
To rise above our pain.

All, all beneath the shining sun
Is vanity and dust;
Help us, O high and holy One,
To fix in Thee our trust;

And in the change, and interfuse
Of change, with every hour,
To recognize the shifting hues
Of never-changing Power.

WHITHER.

ALL the time my soul is calling,
  "Whither, whither do I go?"
For my days like leaves are falling
  From my tree of life below.

Who will come and be my lover!
  Who is strong enough to save,
When that I am leaning over
  The dark silence of the grave?

Wherefore should my soul be calling,
  "Whither, whither do I go?"
For my days like leaves are falling
  In the hand of God, I know.

As the seasons touch their ending,
  As the dim years fade and flee,
Let me rather still be sending
  Some good deed to plead for me.

Then, though none should stay to weep me,
  Lover-like, within the shade,
He will hold me, He will keep me,
  And I will not be afraid.

SURE ANCHOR.

OUT of the heavens come down to me,
  O Lord, and hear my earnest prayer
On life above the life I see
  Fix Thou my soul, and keep it there.

The richest joys of earth are poor;
  The fairest forms are all unfair;
On what is peaceable and pure
  Set Thou my heart, and keep it there.

Pride builds her house upon the sand;
  Ambition treads the spider's stair;
On whatsoever things will stand
  Set Thou my feet, and keep them there.

The past is vanished in the past;
  The future doth a shadow wear;
On whatsoever things are fast
  Fix Thou mine eyes, and keep them there.

In spite of slander's tongue, in spite
  Of burdens grievous hard to bear,
To whatsoever things are right
  Set Thou my hand, and keep it there.

Life is a little troubled breath,
  Love but another name for care ;
Lord, anchor Thou my hope and faith
  In things eternal, — only there.

36

REMEMBER.

In thy time, and times of mourning,
When grief doeth all she can
To hide the prosperous sunshine,
Remember this, O man, —
" He setteth an end to darkness."

Sad saint, of the world forgotten,
Who workest thy work apart,
Take thou this promise for comfort,
And hold it in thy heart, —
" He searcheth out all perfection "

O foolish and faithless sailor,
When the ship is driven away,
When the waves forget their places,
And the anchor will not stay, —
" He weigheth the waters by measure."

O outcast, homeless, bewildered,
Let now thy murmurs be still,
Go in at the gates of gladness
And eat of the feast at will, —
" For wisdom is better than riches."

O diligent, diligent sower,
  Who sowest thy seed in vain,
When the corn in the ear is withered,
  And the young flax dies for rain, —
"Through rocks He cutteth out rivers"

LYRIC.

Thou givest, Lord, to Nature law,
  And she in turn doth give
Her poorest flower a right to draw
  Whate'er she needs to live.

The dews upon her forehead fall,
  The sunbeams round her lean,
And dress her humble form with all
  The glory of a queen.

In thickets wild, in woodland bowers,
  By waysides, everywhere,
The plainest flower of all the flowers
  Is shining with Thy care.

And shall I through my fear and doubt
  Be less than one of these,
And come from seeking Thee without
  Thy blessed influences?

Thou who hast crowned my life with powers
  So large, — so high above
The fairest flower of all the flowers,
  Forbid it by Thy love.

SUNDAY MORNING.

O DAY to sweet religious thought
So wisely set apart,
Back to the silent strength of life
Help thou my wavering heart.

Nor let the obtrusive lies of sense
My meditations draw
From the composed, majestic realm
Of everlasting law.

Break down whatever hindering shapes
I see, or seem to see,
And make my soul acquainted with
Celestial company.

Beyond the wintry waste of death
Shine fields of heavenly light;
Let not this incident of time
Absorb me from their sight.

I know these outward forms wherein
  So much my hopes I stay,
Are but the shadowy hints of that
  Which cannot pass away.

That just outside the work-day path
  By man's volition trod,
Lie the resistless issues of
  The things ordained of God.

IN THE DARK.

OUT of the earthly years we live
  How small a profit springs;
I cannot think but life should give
  Higher and better things.

The very ground whereon we tread
  Is clothed to please our sight;
I cannot think that we have read
  Our dusty lesson right.

So little comfort we receive,
  Except through what we see,
I cannot think we half believe
  Our immortality.

We disallow and trample so
  The rights of poor, weak men,
I cannot think we feel and know
  They are our brethren.

So rarely our affections move
  Without a selfish guard,
I cannot think we know that love
  Is all of love's reward.

To him who smites, the cheek is turned
With such a slow consent,
I cannot think that we have learned
The holy Testament.

Blind, ignorant, we grope along
A path misunderstood,
Mingling with folly and with wrong
Some providential good.

Striving with vain and idle strife
In outward shows to live,
We famish, knowing not that life
Has better things to give.

PARTING SONG.

THE long day is closing,
  Ah, why should you weep?
'T is thus that God gives
  His beloved ones sleep.

I see the wide water
  So deep and so black, —
Love waits me beyond it, —
  I would not go back!

I would not go back
  Where its joys scarce may gleam, —
Where even in dreaming
  We know that we dream;

For though life filled for me
  All measures of bliss,
Has it anything better
  Or sweeter than this?

I would not go back
  To the torment of fear, —
To the wastes of uncomfort
  When home is so near.

Each night is a prison-bar
  Broken and gone, —
Each morning a golden gate,
  On, — farther on!

On, on toward the city
  So shining and fair;
And He that hath loved me —
  Died for me — is there.

MOURN NOT.

O MOURNER, mourn not vanished light,
  But fix your fearful hopes above;
The watcher, through the long, dark night,
  Shall see the daybreak of God's love.

A land all green and bright and fair,
  Lies just beyond this vale of tears,
And we shall meet, immortal there,
  The pleasures of our mortal years.

He who to death has doomed our race,
  With steadfast faith our souls has armed,
And made us children of His grace
  To go into the grave, unharmed.

The storm may beat, the night may close,
  The face may change, the blood run chill,
But His great love no limit knows,
  And therefore we should fear no ill.

Dust as we are, and steeped in guilt,
  How strange, how wondrous, how divine,
That He hath for us mansions built,
  Where everlasting splendors shine.

Our days with beauty let us trim,
  As Nature trims with flowers the sod;
Giving the glory all to Him, —
  Our Friend, our Father, and our God.

THE HEAVEN THAT'S HERE.

My God, I feel Thy wondrous might
  In Nature's various shows, —
The whirlwind's breath, — the tender light
  Of the rejoicing rose.

For doth not that same power enfol
  Whatever things are new,
Which shone about the saints of old
  And struck the seas in two?

Ashamed, I veil my fearful eyes
  From this, Thy earthly reign;
What shall I do when I arise
  From death, but die again!

What shall I do but prostrate fall
  Before the splendor there,
That here, so dazzles me through all
  The dusty robes I wear.

Life's outward and material laws, —
  Love, sunshine, all things bright, —
Are curtains which Thy mercy draws
  To shield us from that light.

I falter when I try to seek
  The world which these conceal;
I stammer when I fain would speak
  The reverence that I feel.

I dare not pray to Thee to give
  That heaven which shall appear;
My cry is, Help me, Thou, to live
  Within the heaven that 's here.

THE STREAM OF LIFE.

THE stream of life is going dry;
Thank God, that more and more
I see the golden sands, which I
Could never see before.

The banks are dark with graves of friends;
Thank God, for faith sublime
In the eternity that sends
Its shadows into time.

The flowers are gone that with their glow
Of sunshine filled the grass;
Thank God, they were but dim and low
Reflections in a glass.

The autumn winds are blowing chill;
The summer warmth is done;
Thank God, the little dew-drop still
Is drawn into the sun.

Strange stream, to be exhaled so fast
In cloudy cares and tears;
Thank God, that it should shine at last
Along the immortal years.

DEAD AND ALIVE.

Till I learned to love Thy name,
  Lord, Thy grace denying,
I was lost in sin and shame,
  Dying, dying, dying!

Nothing could the world impart;
  Darkness held no morrow;
In my soul and in my heart
  Sorrow, sorrow, sorrow!

All the blossoms came to blight;
  Noon was dull and dreary;
Night and day, and day and night,
  Weary, weary, weary!

When I learned to love Thy name,
  Peace beyond all measure
Came, and in the stead of shame,
  Pleasure, pleasure, pleasure!

Winds may beat, and storms may fall,
  Thou, the meek and lowly,
Reignest, and I sing through all, —
  Holy, holy, holy!

Life may henceforth never be
  Like a dismal story,
For beyond its bound I see
  Glory, glory, glory!

INVOCATION.

Come down to us, help and heal us,
  Thou that once life's pathway trod,
Knowing all its gloom and glory, —
  Son of man, and Son of God.

Come down to us, help and heal us,
  When our hopes before us flee;
Thou hast been a man of sorrows,
  Tried and tempted, even as we.

By the weakness of our nature,
  By the burdens of our care,
Steady up our fainting courage, —
  Save, O save us from despair!

By the still and strong temptation
  Of consenting hearts within;
By the power of outward evil,
  Save, O save us from our sin!

By the infirm and bowed together, —
  By the demons far and near, —
By all sick and sad possessions,
  Save, O save us from our fear!

From the dim and dreary doubting
  That with faith a warfare make,
Save us, through Thy sweet compassion, —
  Save us, for Thy own name's sake.

And when all of life is finished
  To the last low fainting breath,
Meet us in the awful shadows,
  And deliver us from death.

LIFE OF LIFE.

To Him who is the Life of life,
  My soul its vows would pay;
He leads the flowery seasons on,
  And gives the storm its way.

The winds run backward to their caves
  At His divine command, —
And the great deep He folds within
  The hollow of His hand.

He clothes the grass, He makes the rose
  To wear her good attire;
The moon He gives her patient grace,
  And all the stars their fire.

He hears the hungry raven's cry,
  And sends her young their food,
And through our evil intimates
  His purposes of good.

He stretches out the north, He binds
  The tempest in His care;
The mountains cannot strike their roots
  So deep He is not there.

Hid in the garment of His works,
  We feel His presence still
With us, and through us fashioning
  The mystery of His will.

MERCIES.

Lest the great glory from on high
  Should make our senses swim,
Our blessèd Lord hath spread the sky
  Between ourselves and Him.

He made the Sabbath shine before
  The work-days and the care,
And set about its golden door
  The messengers of prayer.

Across our earthly pleasures fled
  He sends His heavenly light,
Like morning streaming broad and red
  Adown the skirts of night.

He nearest comes when most His face
  Is wrapt in clouds of gloom;
The firmest pillars of His grace
  Are planted in the tomb.

Oh shall we not the power of sin
  And vanity withstand,
When thus our Father holds us in
  The hollow of His hand?

PLEASURE AND PAIN.

PLEASURE and pain walk hand in hand,
Each is the other's poise;
The borders of the silent land
Are full of troubled noise.

While harvests yellow as the day
In plenteous billows roll,
Men go about in blank dismay,
Hungry of heart and soul.

Like chance-sown weeds they grow, and drift
On to the drowning main;
Oh, for a lever that would lift
Thought to a higher plane!

Sin is destructive: he is dead
Whose soul is lost to truth;
While virtue makes the hoary head
Bright with eternal youth.

There is a courage that partakes
Of cowardice; a high
And honest-hearted fear that makes
The man afraid to lie.

When no low thoughts of self intrude,
  Angels adjust our rights;
And love that seeks its selfish good
  Dies in its own delights.

How much we take, — how little give, —
  Yet every life is meant
To help all lives; each man should live
  For all men's betterment.

MYSTERIES.

Clouds, with a little light between;
  Pain, passion, fear, and doubt, —
What voice shall tell me what they mean?
  I cannot find them out!

Hopeless my task is, to begin,
  Who fail with all my power,
To read the crimson lettering in
  The modest meadow flower.

Death, with shut eyes and icy cheek,
  Bearing that bitter cup;
Oh, who is wise enough to speak,
  And break its silence up!

Or read the evil writing on
  The wall of good, for, oh,
The more my reason shines upon
  Its lines, the less I know:

Or show how dust becomes a rose,
  And what it is above
All mysteries that doth compose
  Discordance into Love.

I only know that Wisdom planned,
  And that it is my part
To trust, who cannot understand
  The beating of my neart.

LYRIC.

Thou givest, Lord, to Nature law,
  And she in turn doth give
Her poorest flower a right to draw
  Whate'er she needs to live.

The dews upon her forehead fall,
  The sunbeams round her lean,
And dress her humble form with all
  The glory of a queen.

In thickets wild, in woodland bowers,
  By waysides, everywhere,
The plainest flower of all the flowers
  Is shining with Thy care.

And shall I, through my fear and doubt,
  Be less than one of these,
And come from seeking Thee without
  Thy blessèd influences?

Thou who hast crowned my life with powers
  So large, — so high above
The fairest flower of all the flowers, —
  Forbid it by Thy love.

TRUST.

Away with all life's memories,
  Away with hopes, away!
Lord, take me up into Thy love,
  And keep me there to-day.

I cannot trust to mortal eyes
  My weakness and my sin;
Temptations He alone can judge,
  Who knows what they have been.

But I can trust Him who provides
  The thirsty ground with dew,
And round the wounded beetle builds
  His grassy house anew.

For the same hand that smites with pain,
  And sends the wintry snows,
Doth mould the frozen clod again
  Into the summer rose.

My soul is melted by that love,
  So tender and so true;
I can but cry, My Lord and God,
  What wilt Thou have me do?

My blessings all come back to me,
  And round about me stand;
Help me to climb their dizzy stairs
  Until I touch Thy hand.

ALL IN ALL.

AWEARY, wounded unto death, —
Unfavored of men's eyes,
I have a house not made with hands,
Eternal, in the skies.

A house where but the steps of faith
Through the white light have trod,
Steadfast among the mansions of
The City of our God.

There never shall the sun go down
From the lamenting day ;
There storms shall never rise to beat
The light of love away.

There living streams through deathless flowers
Are flowing free and wide ;
There souls that thirsted here below
Drink, and are satisfied.

I know my longing shall be filled
When this weak, wasting clay
Is folded like a garment from
My soul, and laid away.

I know it by th' immortal hopes
  That wrestle down my fear, —
By all the awful mysteries
  That hide heaven from us here.

Oh, what a blissful heritage
  On such as I to fall;
Possessed of Thee, my Lord and God,
  I am possessed of all.

THE PURE IN HEART.

"Blessed are the pure in heart, for they shall see God."

I ASKED the angels in my prayer,
 With bitter tears and pains,
To show mine eyes the kingdom where
 The Lord of glory reigns.

I said, My way with doubt is dim,
 My heart is sick with fear;
Oh come, and help me build to Him
 A tabernacle here!

The storms of sorrow wildly beat,
 The clouds with death are chill;
I long to hear His voice so sweet,
 Who whispered, "Peace; be still!"

The angels said, God giveth you
 His love, — what more is ours?
And even as the gentle dew
 Descends upon the flowers,

His grace descends; and, as of old,
  He walks with man apart,
Keeping the promise, as foretold,
  With all the pure in heart.

Thou needst not ask the angels where
  His habitations be;
Keep thou thy spirit clean and fair,
  And He shall dwell with thee.

40

UNSATISFIED.

Come out from heaven, O Lord, and be my guide, —
Come, I implore ;
To my dark questionings unsatisfied,
Leave me no more, —
No more, O Lord, no more!

Forgetting how my nights and how my days
Run sweetly by, —
Forgetting that Thy ways above our ways
Are all so high, —
I cry, and ever cry —

Since that Thou leavest not the wildest glen,
For flowers to wait,
How leavest Thou the hearts of living men
So desolate, —
So darkly desolate?

Thou keepest safe beneath the wintry snow
The little seed,
And leavest under all its weights of woe,
The heart to bleed,
And vainly, vainly plead.

In the dry root Thou stirrest up the sap;
At Thy commands
Cometh the rain, and all the bushes clap
Their rosy hands:
Man only, thirsting, stands.

Is it for envy, or from wrath that springs
From foolish pride,
Thou leavest him to his dark questionings
Unsatisfied,—
Always unsatisfied?

MORE LIFE.

When spring-time prospers in the grass,
And fills the vales with tender bloom,
And light winds whisper as they pass
Of sunnier days to come;

In spite of all the joy she brings
To flood and field, to hill and grove,
This is the song my spirit sings, —
More light, more life, more love!

And when, her time fulfilled, she goes
So gently from her vernal place,
And all the outstretched landscape glows
With sober summer grace;

When on the stalk the ear is set,
With all the harvest promise bright,
My spirit sings the old song yet, —
More love, more life, more light!

When stubble takes the place of grain,
  And shrunken streams steal slow along,
And all the faded woods complain
  Like one who suffers wrong;

When fires are lit, and everywhere
  The pleasures of the household rife,
My song is solemnized to prayer, —
  More love, more light, more life!

LIGHT AND DARKNESS.

Darkness, blind darkness every way,
  With low illuminings of light;
Hints, intimations of the day
  That never breaks to full, clear light.

High longing for a larger light
  Urges us onward o'er life's hill;
Low fear of darkness and of night
  Presses us back and holds us still.

So while to Hope we give one hand,
  The other hand to Fear we lend;
And thus 'twixt high and low we stand,
  Waiting and wavering to the end.

Eager for some ungotten good,
  We mind the false and miss the true;
Leaving undone the things we would,
  We do the things we would not do.

For ill in good and good in ill,
  The verity, the thing that seems, —
They run into each other still,
  Like dreams in truth, like truth in dreams.

Seeing the world with sin imbued,
  We trust that in the eternal plan
Some little drop of brightest blood
  Runs through the darkest heart of man.

Living afar from what is near,
  Uplooking while we downward tend;
In light and shadow, hope and fear,
  We sin and suffer to the end.

SUBSTANCE.

EACH fearful storm that o'er us rolls,
  Each path of peril trod,
Is but a means whereby our souls
  Acquaint themselves with God.

Our want and weakness, shame and sin,
  His pitying kindness prove;
And all our lives are folded in
  The mystery of His love.

The grassy land, the flowering trees,
  The waters, wild and dim, —
These are the cloud of witnesses
  That testify of Him.

His sun is shining, sure and fast,
  O'er all our nights of dread;
Our darkness by His light, at last
  Shall be interpreted.

No promise shall He fail to keep
  Until we see His face;
E'en death is but a tender sleep
  In the eternal race.

Time's empty shadow cheats our eyes,
  But all the heavens declare
The substance of the things we prize
  Is there, and only there.

LIFE'S MYSTERY.

LIFE's sadly solemn mystery
  Hangs o'er me like a weight;
The glorious longing to be free,
  The gloomy bars of fate.

Alternately the good and ill,
  The light and dark, are strung;
Fountains of love within my heart,
  And hate upon my tongue.

Beneath my feet the unstable ground,
  Above my head the skies;
Immortal longings in my soul,
  And death before my eyes.

No purely pure, and perfect good,
  No high, unhindered power;
A beauteous promise in the bud,
  And mildew on the flower.

The glad, green brightness of the spring;
  The summer, soft and warm;
The faded autumn's fluttering gold,
  The whirlwind and the storm.

To find some sure interpreter
  My spirit vainly tries;
I only know that God is love,
  And know that love is wise.

FOR SELF-HELP.

MASTER, I do not ask that Thou
With milk and wine my table spread,
So much, as for the will to plough
And sow my fields, and earn my bread;
Lest at Thy coming I be found
A useless cumberer of the ground.

I do not ask that Thou wilt bless
With gifts of heavenly sort my day,
So much, as that my hands may dress
The borders of my lowly way
With constant deeds of good and right,
Thereby reflecting heavenly light.

I do not ask that Thou shouldst lift
My feet to mountain-heights sublime,
So much, as for the heavenly gift
Of strength, with which myself may climb,
Making the power Thou madest mine
For using, by that use, divine.

I do not ask that there may flow
  Glory about me from the skies;
The knowledge that doth knowledge know;
  The wisdom that is not too wise
To see in all things good and fair,
Thy love attested, is my prayer.

DYING HYMN.

Earth, with its dark and dreadful ills,
  Recedes, and fades away;
Lift up your heads, ye heavenly hills;
  Ye gates of death, give way!

My soul is full of whispered song;
  My blindness is my sight;
The shadows that I feared so long
  Are all alive with light.

The while my pulses faintly beat,
  My faith doth so abound,
I feel grow firm beneath my feet
  The green immortal ground.

That faith to me a courage gives,
  Low as the grave, to go;
I know that my Redeemer lives:
  That I shall live, I know.

The palace walls I almost see,
  Where dwells my Lord and King;
O grave, where is thy victory!
  O death, where is thy sting!

EXTREMITIES.

When the mildew's blight we see
  Over all the harvest spread,
Humbly, Lord, we cry to Thee,
  Give, O give us, daily bread!
But the full and plenteous ears
Many a time we reap with tears.

When the whirlwind rocks the land,
  When the gathering clouds alarm,
Lord, within Thy sheltering hand,
  Hide, O hide us from the storm!
So with trembling souls we cry,
Till the cloud and noise pass by.

When our pleasures fade away,
  When our hopes delusive prove,
Prostrate at Thy feet we pray,
  Shield, O shield us with Thy love!
But, our anxious plea allowed,
We grow petulant and proud.

When life's little day turns dull,
  When the avenging shades begin,
Save us, O Most Merciful,
  Save us, save us from our sin!
So, the last dread foe being near,
We entreat Thee, through our fear.

Ere the dark our light efface,
  Ere our pleasure fleeth far,
Make us worthier of Thy grace,
  Stubborn rebels that we are;
While our good days round us shine,
O our Father, make us Thine.

HERE AND THERE.

HERE is the sorrow, the sighing,
  Here are the cloud and the night;
Here is the sickness, the dying,
  There are the life and the light!

Here is the fading, the wasting,
  The foe that so watchfully waits;
There are the hills everlasting,
  The city with beautiful gates.

Here are the locks growing hoary,
  The glass with the vanishing sands;
There are the crown and the glory,
  The house that is made not with hands.

Here is the longing, the vision,
  The hopes that so swiftly remove;
There is the blessèd fruition,
  The feast, and the fulness of love.

Here are the heart-strings a-tremble,
  And here is the chastening rod;
There is the song and the cymbal,
  And there is our Father and God.

THE DAWN OF PEACE.

AFTER the cloud and the whirlwind,
After the long, dark night,
After the dull, slow marches,
And the thick, tumultuous fight,
Thank God, we see the lifting
Of the golden, glorious light!

After the sorrowful partings,
After the sickening fear,
And after the bitter sealing
With blood, of year to year,
Thank God, the light is breaking;
Thank God, the day is here!

The land is filled with mourning
For husbands and brothers slain,
But a hymn of glad thanksgiving
Rises over the pain;
Thank God, our gallant soldiers
Have not gone down in vain!

The cloud is spent; the whirlwind
  That vexed the night is past;
And the day whose blessed dawning
  We see, shall surely last,
Till all the broken fetters
  To ploughshares shall be cast!

When over the field of battle
  The grass grows green, and when
The Spirit of Peace shall have planted
  Her olives once again,
Oh, how the hosts of the people
  Shall cry, Amen, Amen!

OCCASIONAL.

Our mightiest in our midst is slain;
  The mourners weep around,
Broken and bowed with bitter pain,
  And bleeding through his wound.

Prostrate, o'erwhelmed, with anguish torn,
  We cry, great God, for aid;
Night fell upon us, even at morn,
  And we are sore afraid.

Afraid of our infirmities,
  In this, our woful woe, —
Afraid to breast the bloody seas
  That hard against us flow.

The sword we sheathed, our enemy
  Has bared, and struck us through;
And heart, and soul, and spirit cry,
  What wilt Thou have us do!